Cooperative Care: Seven Steps to Stress-Free Husbandry

Deborah A. Jones, Ph.D.

First published in 2018 by: Deborah A. Jones Ph.D.

Copyright © 2018 Deborah A. Jones Ph.D.

All uncredited photos © 2017 Barb Cerrito

Designed by: Rebeccah Aube | Power Up K9 Design!

Editing: Crystal Barrera

ISBN NUMBER: 978-0-578-42313-5

Table of Contents

About the Author

Deborah Jones, Ph.D. specializes in social and behavioral psychology. She has recently retired after 20 years teaching a variety of psychology classes at Kent State University, and now spends her time focused on animal training. Deb has been a trainer for 25 years working with a huge variety of dog breeds and a large number of other species as well. This is the twelfth book she has written or co-authored, in addition to helping produce several series of training DVDs. Deb currently spends the majority of her time teaching online and giving webinars at Fenzi Dog Sports Academy. Her Cooperative Care online class is a very popular one. In addition to animal training Deb enjoys hiking with her dogs, reading, and traveling.

Acknowledgments

There are many people I would like to thank for their contributions to cooperative care in general and to this book in particular. First, thanks to my friend Denise Fenzi for all her encouragement and help. Also, thanks to all the Fenzi Dog Sports Academy instructors who have inspired me to be a better trainer and improve my skills just to keep up. You guys are an amazing group! Special thanks to my co-instructor Judy Keller for all her support and assistance.

Thanks to Crystal Barrera (editor) and Rebeccah Aube (graphic design) for their exceptional work on this book as well as the Dog Sport Skills series. They make the process so smooth! And huge thanks also goes to Barb Cerrito for her amazing photography work.

My FDSA Cooperative Care students have been a huge source of motivation and inspiration. It has been my pleasure and honor to work with each team as you move towards choice-based husbandry. I have been highly impressed with your desire to help your dogs become more relaxed and comfortable with husbandry procedures.

My initial inspiration for the class, and now this book, came from Ken Ramirez. After spending a week at Shedd Aquarium, I came to see how husbandry, when trained with positive reinforcement, can vastly improve the lives of the animals in our care. To continue the Chicago theme, I'd also like to acknowledge and thank Laura Monaco Torelli, an awesome trainer and all-around lovely human being. Her work with Santino motivated me to do more and be better.

I'd also like to thank my friend Lara Joseph for allowing me to observe and work with her and her menagerie at The Animal Behavior Center. Her strong focus on training as enrichment has definitely changed my approach in my day-to-day work with my own animals.

I truly appreciate being able to work with a groomer, Tricia Solinger, that I trust totally and completely. We also appreciate our vet, Dr. Mary Dubelko, and all the vets and staff at Keystone Veterinary Clinic, for their thoughtfulness and care while handling our animals.

And finally, though we never met, I'd like to thank Sophia Yin, DVM, for all her amazing contributions to both dog training and veterinary care with the concept of low-stress handling. She was a true pioneer in this field.

I have been very lucky to learn from and be inspired by some absolutely fabulous trainers. I am very grateful for the opportunity to add my own small contribution to this area.

Dedication

I would like to dedicate this book to two of our dogs, Quest and Helo. Both were models for many of the photos you see here. Quest is the tri-colored Sheltie and Helo is one of the red tri-colored Border Collies. All of our dogs, and even the cat, were fantastic subjects and made the photography process smooth and easy. We appreciate that they work hard and make us look good!

Sadly, shortly after this photo session Quest and Helo died due to a tragic and traumatic event. They were both greatly loved and are greatly missed every single day. Our lives were forever changed when they left us. We are proud of them and proud to share their work with you in this book.

Introduction

You already know that having dog in your life means caring for that animal with grooming and veterinary procedures, also known as husbandry work. If you're like most people, you treat these tasks as a chore to be performed. If you're lucky, your dog tolerates baths and nail trims and going to the vet. If you're not so lucky, these things can be a major battle, stressful for all involved.

But did you know that it doesn't have to be that way? Zookeepers and trainers who work with a wide variety of domestic and exotic animals have long known that the animals in their care can be trained to cooperate with medical procedures, even painful ones, without being held down, sedated, or forced into compliance. And your dog can learn to cooperate with his care, too!

In this book, I will explain how you can train your dog to participate in his care willingly. Not only will this training help build up your dog's tolerance to potentially unpleasant events, it will also teach you how to give your dog choices. Because I believe it is very important to train in as much of a stress-free manner as possible, whenever possible, your dog will be allowed to opt out of a session if he is feeling nervous or overwhelmed. Granted, there may be times in real life when something simply must be done whether your dog wants it or not, but the goal is always to give your dog the freedom to say when it's time to take a break.

All of my instructions, suggestions, and recommendations are based on solid scientific training techniques using classical conditioning and positive reinforcement. As a behavioral psychologist, I believe it is very important to base training on scientific learning theories and principles. You can have confidence that the instructions in this book are both effective and humane!

This book is primarily a practical, step-by-step guide to this process. First, however, I'd like to spend the rest of the introduction explaining some of the basic ideas behind these steps.

The Importance of Husbandry

Husbandry refers to the procedures that are necessary in order to keep companion animals happy and healthy. The two main types of husbandry are grooming and veterinary care.

It is important for your dog's health and well-being that he is regularly checked for pain, swelling, lumps, or other abnormalities. Doing this requires that you touch your dog's body all over. Further, at some point all animals will need care that they might consider scary or frightening. Husbandry training will help your dog become comfortable with this reality while also lowering stress and anxiety for both of you. Working hard to make those events pleasant and stress free means that your dog will be relaxed and happier - and you will also be more relaxed and happier as a result!

What is Cooperative Care?

I use this term to refer to training and handling techniques that are based on the animal's voluntary cooperation, as opposed to those based on force or pressure. In this book, I will focus on methods that encourage your dog to become an equal partner in the training process rather than being an unwilling subject. Husbandry is something you will do WITH him rather than TO him. This focus on cooperation rather than conflict is at the heart of this book.

Safety First!

It is extremely important to consider safety issues before you begin husbandry work, and at every point during the process. No one should ever be hurt during husbandry training!

The main safety issue to consider has to do with your dog's reactions to being handled. Many dogs have learned that being handled is a bad thing, and that growling, snapping, or biting can make it stop. This is a very big, very dangerous problem. While this book will offer lots of helpful information, my assumption is that your dog will not react with aggression, even if he dislikes being handled or touched. If your dog has a history of aggression, please seek in person guidance from a qualified animal behaviorist before proceeding.

Any animal can become aggressive, especially if severely frightened or in pain. That is why it's very important to constantly monitor your dog's reactions and emotional state during training. If you see any troubling signs, stop what you are doing and seek qualified help.

It's also important to think about safety in terms of the tools you will be using during training. You may be working with sharp objects such as scissors or clippers. You will be working close to your dog's eyes and mouth. Your dog is likely to be up on a high table for many of your training sessions. All of this requires thought and care to be sure that neither of you is accidentally injured.

Always remember, this is YOUR dog and YOUR training. If something is not comfortable for both you and your dog, then don't do it! You should both always have the choice to opt out of anything that makes you uncomfortable, even if I recommend it in this book.

Types of Learning

I will try to restrain my college professor self here and give you short and easy explanations! That's not easy since this is my specialty, but I'll do my best.

Whenever I train a dog, I ask myself two questions. The first is, "How do I want my dog to feel about this?" The second is, "What do I want my dog to do?" Each of these questions addresses a different type of learning.

The first question about feelings and emotions relates to a type of learning known as classical conditioning. Classical conditioning happens naturally. It is the association of an emotion and a reaction with something in the environment. Imagine your reaction to something that you're very afraid of, perhaps spiders. When you see a spider, you have an automatic startle response. You don't have time to think between the stimulus (spider) and the response (startle). It happens to you. That's the basis of this type of learning. For example, many dogs are afraid of the nail clippers. I'm sure you didn't set out to teach your dog to be afraid of the clippers, it just happened, and classical conditioning is how. The clippers have been associated with something unpleasant and now take on an unpleasant connotation themselves.

The good news is that you can use classical conditioning to change these responses. The bad news is that this type of training, often referred to as counterconditioning, is likely to take a lot longer than the initial learning. Counterconditioning is accomplished by exposing our dogs to the feared object, action, or situation at a very mild level and following each exposure with a positive event (in our case, food).

Changing an automatic reaction is not easy. If exposure to the feared stimulus is too intense, it will actually set the training back. Therefore, it is important to move forward in tiny steps, or even to move backwards when your dog needs you to do that. I will talk about the specifics involved as they come up

So how do I want my dog to feel about what we're doing? The answer is pretty much always GREAT! I want my dog to love what we're doing together. I want it to be fun and interesting and enjoyable. I DON'T want it to be confusing or scary or unpleasant.

It takes very few repetitions to learn to be afraid of an object (like nail clippers) or a specific situation (the vet's office, for example). Just one or two unpleasant experiences is enough. This means that I will be constantly monitoring my dog's reactions and responses. There are certain tell-tale signs of discomfort. Some dogs are obvious about it and leave. But some are much more subtle. There may be a tongue flick here or slightly flattened ears there; things you could easily miss if you aren't paying attention.

It pays to observe your dog carefully during husbandry training sessions. While he may be allowing you to do something to him, that doesn't mean he's comfortable. If you continue to try to work despite his discomfort, things will get worse. Take any signs that seem to indicate concern or anxiety as important feedback. Your dog is telling you something very important and you really should listen.

The second question - "What do I want my dog to do?" - relates to a type of learning known as operant conditioning. This type of learning happens when you teach your dog that performing specific behaviors leads to something he desires (usually a tasty cookie). Doing something that you teach him to do leads to a happy outcome.

Husbandry work often requires your dog to move into certain positions and then hold still in those positions while a variety of procedures

You can see Star's discomfort with restraint in this photo. She shows wide open eyes with lots of white showing on one side (often called whale eye), in addition to sticking out her tongue and lip licking. Her body is also tense and tight. She tolerates this handling but clearly dislikes it.

In this photo, Judy is restraining Quest quite firmly, but he is calm and relaxed. Look at his eyes, ears, and mouth. All are indicating a neutral reaction. Compared to Star's picture, you can see a huge difference!

are performed. This can be accomplished with operant conditioning, which works best when you have a training plan that is broken down into many tiny steps. By training each desired behavior in a thoughtful manner, you can successfully teach a variety of useful husbandry actions.

The Importance of Choice

Throughout this book, I will focus again and again on the importance of giving animals a choice, which means they can leave training sessions if they choose. This idea might be pretty scary for some folks. Giving up control of the sessions and allowing a dog to have an equal say in what happens is hard, but animals who are given a choice often choose to opt in and cooperate.

What do you do if your dog decides to leave a session? Take that feedback seriously and consider why your dog felt the need to leave. It's likely that something was happening that made him uncomfortable; dogs have no reason to disengage and leave when they are comfortable.

Because I have allowed my own dogs free choice, they are eager to be the one who gets to be on the grooming table. They have a huge reinforcement history for cooperating with me and being groomed. In fact, they now consider being allowed on the grooming table to be a huge reward. This is the kind of attitude and behavior that I want to establish! And I got it by giving my dogs the opportunity to leave a session. They rarely take that opportunity, but if they do, that's fine. I will learn from it and form a new plan for future sessions.

Years ago I was into horses. One thing anyone who has ever owned a horse knows is that getting a reluctant horse to go in a trailer can be a dangerous process. Horses who are not properly prepared will panic and fight, and you can easily end up with injuries and trauma to both the horse and the people involved.

What if the horse was allowed to leave the trailer whenever he got scared? You might think that he would just never go in. However, if you used operant conditioning to teach the horse to move closer and closer to the trailer in small steps, then the horse would be highly reinforced for moving first towards and then in the trailer. By also keeping classical conditioning in mind and allowing the horse to back off whenever he feels it is necessary, in a surprisingly short time you will have a horse who enters the trailer willingly.

Of course, there are situations in which an animal has no choice because something must get done now. For example, a dog who is injured must be treated whether he likes it or not. Unfortunately, doing this erodes the dog's trust and weakens the relationship with his trainer. It also means the dog will require even more training once the situation has passed. This is often the case when it comes to trimming nails. Even though the goal is for cooperative care, it's often not possible to allow nails to go uncared for during the training period. When you come upon these situations, do what you have to do, in as neutral a manner as possible, then get back to training mode. Know that you are adding to your husbandry work when you do this. It's not ideal, but that's real life.

Some people will argue that all this positive training stuff just takes too long, and to that I say that it takes as long as it takes. Any husbandry training you do is a benefit to you and your dog. The more time you spend focused on allowing your dog to make decisions and positively reinforcing desired choices, the happier both you and your dog will be. Even short training sessions lead you closer to your goals.

Increasing Tolerance

Although giving dogs the choice to cooperate often leads to enjoyment of an activity, for certain things, simple tolerance will be enough. It's just not realistic for a dog to enjoy every husbandry task. This certainly doesn't happen with humans! For example, most people do not find going to the dentist to be fun. It's a chore we do because we must. Although a few of us might actively resist going, most of us simply tolerate the dentist, even if we don't love going. And that's okay.

Likewise, just tolerating a procedure might be enough for your dog. If you are reading this book, it is likely that there are things your dog actively dislikes and resists. These are the tasks we want your dog to begin to tolerate. If you are starting with a puppy or a dog who doesn't have strong negative feelings about handling, then you are in an excellent position. You can work on teaching him to enjoy those procedures. But if your dog has already had unpleasant experiences, you will be starting from a negative position. It will take longer, and you will need to work harder, but big changes ARE possible.

If your dog is nervous and anxious about being handled or having procedures done, you will need to move slowly and carefully through your initial training steps. If your dog seems to be getting worse, stop and reevaluate your approach. Typically, if tolerance levels are not improving, it's because you are pushing too hard and need to back up and make things easier for your dog.

Reinforcers

In order to be successful with both classical and operant conditioning, you need to have valuable reinforcers that your dog will work to obtain. If you don't have anything that your dog wants, then you will not be able to train him.

Most husbandry training will work best with food reinforcers. Food has many advantages here. It is easy to provide, which allows you to get in a large number of repetitions in a very short time. It is also less exciting than toys and play, which will be useful for keeping your dog calm and relaxed while training.

It's a good idea to have several different food reinforcers that you use solely for husbandry work. These should be high value for your dog. I recommend having two types: something soft and easy to spread out such as cheese in a can, meat-flavored baby food, or peanut butter; and treats that are small, soft, and easy to swallow.

If your dog really likes his regular food, you can use it for husbandry training, but most dogs do best with something special, at least for the procedures they dislike. In any case, you'll likely want to cut down a bit on regular meals so your dog doesn't gain weight while doing husbandry training.

What if your dog normally likes food but won't take it while you are training for husbandry behaviors? This should be a big red flag! A dog's unwillingness to eat food is very important information. It's likely that you are pushing too hard and trying to work in a place that makes your dog uncomfortable. Slow down or even take a step or two backwards.

Remote Reinforcement Devices

I have found remote reinforcement devices to be very useful tools for husbandry work. The two most common devices are the Pet Tutor and the Treat & Train. These devices have a small remote control that allows you to release treats. This can be a faster way to deliver the goodies while also allowing you to work at a distance from where your dog receives the food. I also really like the fact that it gives your dog something specific to focus on - the machine - during the training process.

Star on the grooming table with the Pet Tutor™.

These devices are not necessary in order to accomplish good training, but they can be helpful. When I am working on classical conditioning, for example, I can show my dog a tool, then immediately hit the remote to provide cookies. This pairing can be repeated very quickly so learning tends to happen very quickly as well.

Training Sessions

The most important thing to keep in mind when planning training sessions is to keep them short. How short? Shorter than you imagine! Ideally, you would do frequent two minute training sessions. It's fine to do a session, take a short break, then do another, and repeat. But the break is very important. Your dog needs to be able to relax between sessions to clear his head and lower any possible stress that is building up. Then he'll be ready to start fresh again.

Frequent sessions are much more likely to contribute to success than the occasional long one. Taking a few minutes several times a day to train will lead to great progress. Consistency matters. You'll see the most improvement if you stay on a regular training schedule. If you skip a day here or there, that's no big deal. But if one missed day leads to another and then another, your progress will stall. Keep the momentum going!

Training Steps

The remainder of this book is organized by steps. I STRONGLY suggest that you follow the steps in order. You may be tempted to jump ahead to the step where you are having issues, but the first three steps in particular will set you up for success in all your future husbandry training. Skipping over them, or moving through them very quickly, means that you lose a lot of benefit. As with many things, thoroughly working through the foundation steps will pay off quite well in the long run.

I recently took the cooperative care class with my very anxious Mini Aussie. He hated all forms of husbandry from brushing to blood draws prior to this class. He had been deemed the most dramatic patient at the vet clinic and often required sedation for very minor procedures. He has come so far in such a short period of time! He not only is no longer hiding from me when I pull out a brush, but actually approaching and willingly allowing grooming. The most amazing thing though was our most recent vet visit where he stood for a blood draw with zero restraint! I never thought we would accomplish so much so fast. We worked very hard to get there and thanks to Deb and Judy we did!

~ JoAnna Ferraris

Cooperative Care: Case Studies

You've likely bought this book for one of two reasons. One, you have a serious ongoing husbandry training issue that you've been unable to resolve. Or two, you want to be proactive and get the best possible start on a lifetime of pleasant husbandry interactions. In either case, thanks for buying the book! I really do hope you find the help and information you are seeking here. Your efforts will be worthwhile. Over and over again I've seen the value of making the effort to improve our dog's attitude towards and comfort with husbandry work.

You're here reading this book because you're a caring owner and trainer, and it distresses you to see your dog in distress. This is an excellent step in the right direction! Educating yourself and seeking out detailed information about solid science based positive reinforcement training is exactly what you need to do.

My goal with this book is to help clarify and simplify information for you. As the human half of the training team you have the harder job here. You will learn how the two main types of learning (classical and operant) contribute to the issues you are having; and also how they can be used to help change the situation. You will consider all the factors that led you to this place so you don't repeat those unintentional mistakes. Then you will synthesize the new ideas you may learn here and put them into action. And once you do all that, your dog's behavior and attitude will reflect that learning and those changes.

I have provided a step by step holistic approach for this. It really isn't possible to just separate out the "problem" from the larger picture of a dog who is not tolerant of basic handling and procedures. As with everything in animal training, typically the way forward is to go back to basics and build a better foundation.

Before we get into the 'meat' of this book, how to work on improving your dog's tolerance and cooperation for husbandry procedures, I'd like you to take a look at some typical issues that I see and hear about all the time. These case studies are representative of a huge variety of possible challenges that we can encounter. I would like to thank the trainers who responded to my request for case studies. You guys are amazing! Members of Fenzi Dog Sports Alumni group and the Cooperative Care with Deb Jones Facebook groups have been very generous in supplying me with their training challenges for inclusion in this book. It's not easy to share your struggles with the world, so they are both brave AND caring in sharing this information.

For each case I am providing you with some basic information about the dog and the issue. I have summarized in some cases. As you read through the book keep these cases in mind and try to identify information that would be useful to help improve these situations. At the end of the book I will discuss the treatments that the owner has tried, how they have or haven't worked, and then provide my recommendations.

Case #1: Bodhi, German Shepherd Dog, 3 ½ years old

When did you first realize you had an issue with husbandry?

He appeared to have an ear infection and is the only dog ever to not let me put medication in his ear.

What, exactly, did you first notice?

The medication didn't hurt him because it never got near him. He noticed me getting the medicine and somehow figured this was for him and no way no how was he going to let me put something in his sore ear. He ran and hid under my desk. Another time I tried straddling him and he bucked me off. He will let me give him oral medications no problem, but no one is going near that left ear.

*Photo courtesy of Lila Hlebichuk

Case #2: Moses, Rhodesian Ridgeback, 1 year old

When did you first realize you had an issue with husbandry?

Around 10 weeks of age.

What, exactly, did you first notice?

Unfortunately Moses had an allergic reaction to a vaccine he received the day before we brought him home and so we had to give him liquid benadryl at the instruction of our vet. He did NOT like this and I think it set us up for a rough road of husbandry. Pretty much right away he didn't like us handling his head, and I think it goes back to that benadryl on day one of being in our house. Thankfully we have been successful with husbandry regarding feet, but anything with the head is a no go. Of course, I tried to do all the things they tell you to do with a puppy: check the ears, check teeth and gums, etc... but I could tell these caused him distress. He would jerk his head away and create distance between us, so I stopped working on it altogether because I didn't want to create more stress around handling with a young pup.

*Photo courtesy of Alisa Healy

Case #3: Maddie, Mastiff/Boxer mix, 7 years old

When did you first realize you had an issue with husbandry?

In hindsight, she made it clear she did not want strangers taking her temperature rectally from the very first vet appointment I took her to, a few weeks after adopting her. I knew nothing about dogs or behavior at the time, and it didn't seem like a big deal when, after taking her in the back, they reported that "she didn't like the thermometer and tried to alligator roll to get away."

After almost a year (and several more similarly unpleasant vet experiences), she needed a blood draw. The techs had to bring her back out to me to muzzle her, and she continued to thrash around trying to escape the whole time. That was the first time I really witnessed how upset she was, and I started seriously looking into solutions then.

What, exactly, did you first notice?

Over several months, it became clear that she wasn't comfortable with overly interactive strangers in general, and her reactions escalated at unpleasant vet appointments.

She has zero personal space bubble with people she trusts, and doesn't mind being loomed over, paw handling, nail trimming, rear-end wiping, or even blood draws from "her" people. I continue to feed high value treats after any of that to maintain her cooperation.

Basically, her attitude is that her trusted human friends can do pretty much anything to her, and strangers who want to interact are by default a threat.

*Photo courtesy of Linnell Randall

Case #4: Victor, Chihuahua, 3 years old

When did you first realize you had an issue with husbandry?

He was prone to biting from the start if he was uncomfortable with handling (loves being petted, but try to lead him by the collar and you would be bitten).
He was ok at the first vet visit (nothing invasive happened) but on visit 2, I was told that I had to bring him back sedated so they could do a blood draw.
We have made not much progress with this other than to train up a muzzle so that the procedure can be quick and nobody bleeds.

What, exactly, did you first notice?

He goes from zero to fighting hard as soon as he feels frightened or uncomfortable.

*Photo courtesy of Robin Murray

Case #5: Rusty, Boykin Spaniel, 9 years old

When did you first realize you had an issue with husbandry?

Since he was a young dog (probably around 2 years old).

What, exactly, did you first notice?

At that time, I was having a groomer do his nails (he was my first dog and I hadn't learned how to cut nails yet). I honestly didn't realize he needed his nails trimmed so often so he was only getting them done every few months. Watching him at the groomer, he would pull his feet away from them for nail trims. Gradually it got worse to where they could barely trim them because he was flailing around so much. I decided to start doing them myself because I did not like seeing him in distress at the groomer.

*Photo courtesy of Christine Vinciguerra

Step One:
Place Conditioning

It is important to have a dedicated place in your home where you will practice the majority of your husbandry work. You want somewhere that your dog can easily recognize as a husbandry training location and that you don't use for any other purpose. This enables your dog to make decisions about whether or not he wants to participate, as well as understand what he can expect from you.

A grooming table is an ideal place. It is clearly recognizable to your dog as a training place and the height will keep you from ending up with a backache from bending over. If you don't have a grooming table, any elevated surface, such as an ottoman, can work. Choose a surface that is solid, sturdy, stable, large enough for your dog to easily lie down, and that has a non-slip surface. Your dog will be spending a lot of training time there so it should be as comfortable as possible. The most important aspect of your training place is that you set it up so your dog has a way to get on and off by himself. This is what gives him the ability to leave if he's uncomfortable. You can set up your table next to a chair or other piece of furniture to make it possible for your dog to jump up and down safely.

Occasionally, using an elevated surface simply doesn't make sense. For example, maybe you have a giant breed dog. In this case, it's a good idea to set aside a location with a specific floor covering to delineate the space. A foam yoga mat or some children's play tiles would make a good floor covering for your place. Again, make sure the area is large enough for your dog to lie down comfortably.

Loving the Training Place

It is important that your dog loves being in his training place, so once you have defined your training space, it's time to convince your dog that it is the best place he could ever imagine being. This will be done with pure classical conditioning. Your dog does not have to DO anything in particular, you are simply working to make sure he is in the best emotional state possible while in the training place. There are two exercises to accomplish this.

Cheese Bowl

A cheese bowl is a small bowl with food smeared inside for your dog to lick. Although it's called a cheese bowl, you can use any food that your dog will enjoy, such as canned squeeze cheese, meat-flavored baby food, or peanut butter. You could also blend up your own meat mixture if you like. You will want to use this reinforcer sparingly, spreading a thin layer into the bowl and adding more as needed.

Set up your training place so your dog can climb on and off it on his own. Then prepare your cheese bowl. Show your dog the bowl, invite him to the training place, and when he's there, present him with the bowl. Let him lick it all up. Feel free to praise and pet him while he's doing this, but don't be too distracting. Once he's done licking, invite him to leave the place while you refill the bowl. Repeat this sequence three or four times per session.

That's it! Your dog is not required to do anything except lick the food out of the bowl. The goal of this exercise is for your dog to make the association between a specific place and a very special treat.
Repeat these sessions multiple times per day if possible. The more often you do this, the better all future training will go.

Baby Food Syringe

In addition to the cheese bowl you can also provide a special treat to your dog on the table using a large syringe and allowing your dog to lick the food off the tip. As your dog licks you can slowly depress the plunger to provide a steady stream of good stuff.

We use jars of meat-flavored baby food for this, but you can use any food that is thin enough to suck up into the syringe and then dispense easily. Begin with the plunger completely down and place the tip of the syringe into the food. Then slowly pull up the plunger to pull food into the syringe. Then let your dog lick the tip while you slowly depress the plunger. That's it! This method of providing a special treat is sure to make a huge impression with your dog.

Follow the instructions for the cheese bowl above. After several days of multiple repetitions of this on the table your dog should be insistent on being there.

Rapid-Fire Treats

After several days of working with the cheese bowl and baby food
syringe, you can move to rapid-fire treats. Prepare your training
location and obtain thirty small (as small as possible) soft treats.
Ideally, these treats will be something that your dog will love and that
he can swallow very quickly and easily.

Have ten treats ready, then invite your dog to his training place and feed
him those ten treats, one after the other, as quickly as possible. When
the treats are gone, tell him he's all done and encourage him to leave
the place. Prepare another ten treats and wait close to your training
location. If your dog returns on his own, follow the same process of
feeding the ten treats as quickly as possible, then releasing him. If he
does not return on his own, you can gently encourage him. Finally,
prepare the last ten treats, wait again (encourage your dog back only
if necessary), and repeat. After the third round, you are done for this
session.

The goal with rapid-fire treats is for your dog to learn that moving
into the training area will make you start the feeding process. You
can do two to three sessions a day. After a few days your dog should
start eagerly moving towards the training area whenever given the
opportunity.

My students have reported that they will randomly find their dogs
waiting in the training place, hoping that they will be noticed so that
rapid-fire treats will start! If this happens to you, it means you are
definitely doing it right!

If all goes well, within a week you will have classically conditioned
your dog to LOVE your chosen training area. Excellent job! However,
it never hurts to randomly go back to either of these exercises to
continue to build value for the training place throughout the rest of the
training process. Also, if your dog ever has an unpleasant experience in

the training area, such as falling off the table, stop all other work and go back to this step for a week.

Step 1 checklist for Place Conditioning:

- ❑ Dedicated grooming area has been clearly defined

- ❑ Cheese bowl practice in grooming area

- ❑ Baby food syringe in grooming area

- ❑ Rapid-fire treats in grooming area

- ❑ Dog LOVES grooming area!

I took Deb & Judy's Cooperative Care online course through the Fenzi Academy at the Gold level and loved the course. With my previous dogs, desensitizing them to being handled was one of those things that I glossed over and then paid the price when my dogs needed to be handled for procedures and they weren't very cooperative! With my young Border Collie Lulu, I decided to be a better owner and really take the time to make her comfortable with all the ways she might have to be handled one day. The Cooperative Care course was exactly what I needed to help me with that goal. Everything was very well explained and broken down into manageable pieces. Lulu's comfort level with being handled has definitely increased and I was very pleased with the course.

~ Sylvie Fefer

Step Two:
Impulse Control

For much of your husbandry work, you will encourage your dog to be passive and still. This is a very foreign concept for some dogs! Luckily, you can do something about this. By teaching your dog some impulse control exercises, he will learn that holding still is all he needs to do in order to get reinforced, and along the way he will develop a calmer body and mind.

These exercises work by helping your dog understand that waiting for something is in his best interest. This is quite counterintuitive for most dogs AND most people. Usually if a dog wants something, he simply takes it. Now the rule is if he wants something, he has to wait for you to give it to him. By holding still and controlling his urges, he will get what he wants. On the other hand, if he gives in to his impulses and tries to take the food, it will become unavailable. Most dogs figure this out VERY quickly.

Please note that making eye contact with you is NOT a part of any of these exercises. In fact, eye contact may end up being problematic for future training, so please don't ever wait for eye contact before marking and reinforcing. The target behavior is stillness. Reinforce that.

Markers

Before beginning impulse control work, you will need to introduce several different markers. A marker is a unique sound that indicates the dog is performing the desired behavior and that a reinforcer will follow. For the husbandry work described in this book, the reinforcer will be a treat.

It's important to have two unique and specific markers for this work.

One marker for calm, stationary behaviors and passive handling work, and another to indicate permission to move to take the reinforcer. I encourage the use of verbal markers for husbandry training for two reasons. First, many people have already used a clicker for a variety of of behaviors in a variety of situations. While that's great for general training, for husbandry training, you need markers that have a clearly specified contextual meaning. Second, because husbandry exercises are often hands-on, you will not have a hand free to use a clicker. If you move your hand to use a clicker, your click will happen after the behavior, not during it, which will slow down your progress.

Calm Marker

The calm marker is something you only use when you want your dog to be calm and relaxed. You should use this marker when your dog is being still or cooperative, then provide a treat for your dog. Your dog should not have to move to get the treat, you should take it directly to him. This reinforces the notion of being still.

Choose a one syllable word that is easy to say in a low tone. I use the word "good," but "nice" is another common choice. Some folks even choose "calm." You can drag it out a bit so it's more of a "gooood" or "niiiiiice" or "caaaaaalm." Just be sure it's not a word you use often in everyday life.

Everything about the marker and your treat delivery should be calm. Use a low, quiet voice and move slowly. Provide a treat after each marker, but you don't have to rush. Make your movements slow and steady.

The Active Release Marker

An active release is a different type of marker that means the dog can go ahead and get the thing he wants. A typical active release is something like "get it!" Whatever word or short phrase you choose should be quick, sharp, and distinctly different from your calm marker.

When using an active release marker, your dog should immediately break out of position and take the treat. Some dogs may be hesitant to move at first, particularly if you've been doing a lot of impulse control and handling work with a calm marker. It's okay to add some verbal encouragement if necessary.

It's also a good idea to balance out the two different types of work. Alternate four or five repetitions with the calm marker and then an active release marker. This helps your dog learn that he needs to concentrate and listen carefully. If your dog has difficulty with stationary work and controlling himself, do more work with the calm marker. If you see tension or anxiety beginning to develop, an active release can help decrease that by giving your dog a chance to move and clear his head a bit.

Impulse Control Exercises

Introduce these exercises on the floor away from the table or designated training area. This way, if there is any confusion or misunderstanding during initial training, it is not connected with the space you've worked so hard to make your dog love. You can work on these exercises while also doing your place conditioning. Just be sure to separate the sessions both in time and space.

Once your dog begins to show an understanding of an exercise, you can move it to your training spot. Go back to the early steps of training for a quick review when you do this. Going back to baby steps and building up the exercise again helps to keep you from expecting too much, which could cause your dog to fail. Also, if your dog has two failures in a row, the exercise is too hard. The next repetition MUST be successful, so you'll have to make it very easy to ensure success. Then start building up challenge levels again.

Slow Treats

Begin by holding a treat in your hand, make sure your dog sees it, and then hold your hand up at shoulder height. If your dog moves to try to get the treat, hold still and wait. The second your dog stops moving, use your calm marker and deliver the treat to him. Try to get it to your dog before he jumps up for it - but don't worry about it too much. Continue doing this until your dog immediately holds still when he sees you lift the treat up to your shoulder.

Next start moving the treat slowly down towards your dog. At first, an inch is enough. Use your calm marker and then deliver the treat to him. Your goal is to move the treat closer and closer to your dog before marking and delivering the treat. If your dog moves toward the treat before you use your marker, smoothly move the treat back up to your shoulder, wait for him to settle, and then start the process again. Your dog needs to learn that if he holds still, the treat will come to him, but if he moves towards the treat, it goes away.

Remember to follow the two mistakes rule here. If your dog makes a mistake twice in a row, then the exercise is too difficult for your dog! Make it easy enough for him to succeed on the next repetition.

Once your dog understands the concept of slow treats, it can be combined with a large number of husbandry procedures discussed later in this book. This exercise gives your dog something interesting to focus on and a clear way to "win" and is very useful during veterinary exams and grooming.

When you move slow treats to the table, you have a useful tool to help your dog focus and remain still until given permission to take the treat.

Zen Bowl

The zen bowl is a highly useful tool for husbandry work. It can be any bowl, there's nothing special about the bowl itself. The importance is how you train your dog to react to the bowl. Once your dog understands this exercise, you will be able to keep an open bowl of food out while you are training, which makes it easier for you to access the treats. The bowl also serves as both a focal point for your dog and a reminder to exhibit impulse control.

The zen bowl is trained in the same way as the slow treat exercise. Put a treat into the bowl, ensuring that your dog sees you do this. Hold the bowl at shoulder height and wait for your dog to settle. When he does, use your calm marker and move the bowl into your dog so he can access the treat. Continue on until you can move the bowl directly in front of your dog's face before you mark and give him the treat.

Once your dog is successful with that step, you can move the bowl towards the floor, but remember to do so inch by inch. Once your dog is successfully holding still while you lower the bowl to the floor, you can alternate using the calm marker with a delivered treat (bowl moves to dog) and using an active release to the bowl (dog moves to bowl). Some dogs do well while you move the bowl to the floor, but dive in once you move your hand away from it. Watch for this issue. Move your hand away from the bowl in a series of small steps rather than just quickly moving it away.

Please note that in this picture Deb is very carefully moving her hand away from the bowl before marking and reinforcing.

When you can place the bowl on the floor, work on increasing the length of time your dog must wait before you mark and treat or release.

Zen Hand

For this impulse control exercise you will practice first holding food in a closed fist, and then once your dog understands that he needs to back off, be still, and wait for your marker, you will hold the food in your open palm.

 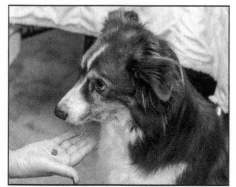

We follow the same basic process for the zen hand exercises as we did for the zen bowl. Hold the food in your closed fist and wait for your dog to settle. When he does, mark, open your hand, and move the treat to him. When this exercise is easy then you can add the challenge of having your hand open with the food in your palm from the beginning. If your dog moves towards your hand you can quickly close it and wait. When he backs away, mark, open your hand, and move the food to him.

The ability to work with your dog while there is an open bowl of food nearby is a great advantage for your husbandry work. This not only gives your dog a focal point but it also allows you to more easily access and provide treats.

Once your dog is doing well with the zen exercises on the ground then it's time to move them to the table or grooming area. Remember, when you change locations make the exercises easier because the change of location itself is enough of an extra challenge. So lower your expectations and then build them back up as your dog is successful.

Food on the Floor

The next variation on the impulse control theme involves food placed directly on the floor (or on the surface of your training area). Follow the same process as with slow treats and zen bowl work. Show your dog the food, hold it at your shoulder height, and slowly begin lowering it to the floor. Work on this in a series of steps making sure your dog can be successful before you make things harder.

As with the zen bowl, you can use your calm marker and deliver the treat to your dog until you get to the point where you place the food on the floor. Then you can add in an active release to the food for some of the repetitions.

Many dogs find food on the floor much more challenging than food in a zen bowl. Somehow that piece of food sitting out there uncontained makes it much harder to maintain control. If your dog loses control and lunges for the

food without being marked, remove the food if possible, move it back up to shoulder height, and begin again. If your dog beats you to the food, there's nothing to be done about it. These things happen. However, it does mean that your dog wasn't quite prepared for the challenge you gave him, so go back to some easier repetitions. It's important that this mistake does not happen repeatedly!

Mat Target

For this exercise, you will be teaching your dog to seek out a mat or bed and then to lie down, relax, and stay on it. The mat can be very useful as a comfortable and familiar place for your dog, and it's portable, too! Being able to take it to the vet's office with you gives your dog a "home away from home." The goal is for the mat to become a portable "happy place" for your dog.

Choose your mat or bed with care. You'll want to be sure that the mat is large enough that your dog can lie down with his entire body on the mat. It's not a bad idea to use something with a non-skid backing so it won't slip on metal tables or tile floors at the vet. Finally, you want the mat to be special, so pick it up and put it away when you're not training with it.

To begin training, put the mat on the ground. When your dog looks at or approaches the mat, mark and toss a treat on the mat for him to get. By reinforcing on the mat, you will make it seem like a very good place for your dog to hang out. If he stays on the mat once he eats the treat, go ahead and mark and treat again, and again, and again.

Once your dog is hanging out on the mat, you can start dropping the treat between his front legs. This usually encourages a dog to lie down to get the treat, and then you can reinforce that position by marking and dropping more treats between his front legs.

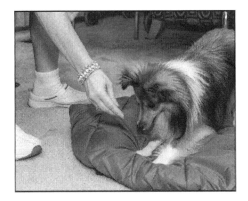 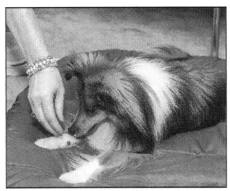

This training process is similar to the rapid-fire treats you did on the table or training area. You can rapidly reinforce eight to ten times, then toss a treat to release your dog from the mat. It's highly likely he'll come back and you can start reinforcing on the mat again. As your dog begins to spend more and more time on the mat, you can slow down the pace of your treats so that's there's a bit of duration happening between each mark/treat.

Final Thoughts on Impulse Control

Impulse control can be a very challenging thing for some dogs to learn. It can be frustrating for both the dog and the trainer when the dog doesn't seem to get it.

When dogs get tired or overwhelmed, impulse control is one of the first things to go, so sticking to short training sessions is incredibly important! If you are having a lot of trouble in a session, just end it. Try again the next day when your dog is fresh.

Your execution of the impulse control exercises is very important. Small mistakes in timing can lead to a lack of progress, or even regression. Before you blame your dog, take a look at your own mechanics. It is very easy to make a number of small errors that impede progress. If possible, find a good trainer to observe you and give feedback or videotape your sessions and watch with a critical eye.

Once you have established the impulse control exercises both on the floor and then in your training place, it's time to move to some handling work.

Step 2 checklist for Impulse Control:

❑ Calm marker introduced

❑ Active release marker introduced

❑ Slow treats on floor and in grooming area

❑ Zen bowl on floor and in grooming area

❑ Closed Zen hand on floor and in grooming area

❑ Open Zen hand on floor and in grooming area

❑ Food on floor on floor and in grooming area

❑ Mat target on floor and in grooming area

Step Three:
General Body Handling

Now that your dog has learned basic impulse control, it's time for some general body handling. This step is a series of a passive exercises in which your dog doesn't have to do much except allow you to touch and move his body. Your dog should learn that things that might normally be unpleasant or frightening are actually tolerable, maybe even worthwhile!

Because the goal is for your dog to become comfortable with your handling, as you complete these exercises, be alert for signs of discomfort. You know your dog. You can tell when he's happy and comfortable and when he's becoming nervous and uneasy. Slow down and go back to some easier work if you sense a problem developing.

All touch-based exercises should be started at a very mild and gentle level. It should seem like a tiny little thing, hardly worth noticing. Then, as your dog becomes accustomed to a particular type of touch or movement, you can gradually increase the intensity level. Gradually is the key word here! Most regression happens when people try to do too much too soon. I'm sure you remember the children's story of the tortoise and the hare. Be the tortoise! Slow and steady truly does win the race here.

Working on your dog's tolerance for general body handling should be completed in two parts. First, as with the impulse control exercises, the initial training should begin on the ground and NOT in your designated training place. You've spent a lot of time making the designated training place a totally fabulous place to be, so establishing this foundation in a separate location is important in case things don't go well with the handling exercises. After you've done the groundwork, you can then move to the table or training space and repeat the exercises there. Start from the very beginning and repeat the entire exercise starting with baby steps.

Be sure to introduce the handling exercises in order, completing each one fully before moving on to the next one.

Stroking

Stroking is a great place to start because it is similar to petting, which makes it familiar and enjoyable for most dogs. Begin with whatever part of your dog's body seems to be the least sensitive. For many dogs this may be the shoulders, back, or hips. Stroke your dog lightly, use your calm marker while you're still stroking, then give your dog a treat.

All your dog has to do is hold still and allow the stroking to happen, but in the initial stages, your dog doesn't need to hold totally still. If he moves away, go ahead and mark and treat anyway. Keep the intensity of your touch very low. After four to five repetitions, most dogs will understand the pattern and begin to hold still. Try to avoid talking to your dog other than the use of the calm marker. If you feel that your dog really needs you to reassure him, you can do that, but keep it as brief and quiet as possible and fade it out as soon as possible.

As you stroke different areas of your dog's body, you will find that he is much more sensitive about some areas than about others. This is perfectly normal. A dog may be fine with stroking on his head, shoulders, and chest, but not at all happy about stroking on his hips or down his back legs. Some dogs have become protective of certain body parts through anxiety and concern, while others may be experiencing physical pain. As a result, you should systematically touch and rate your dog's responses to the following areas:

- ☐   Top and sides of head
- ☐   Ears
- ☐   Neck
- ☐   Chest
- ☐   Shoulders
- ☐   Front legs
- ☐   Front feet
- ☐   Back along spine
- ☐   Sides along ribs
- ☐   Belly
- ☐   Groin area
- ☐   Hips
- ☐   Back legs
- ☐   Back feet
- ☐   Tail

Use this 1 to 5 rating system as you touch each area:

1 = loves
2 = likes
3 = tolerates
4 = dislikes
5 = hates

Doing this simple body scan will help you see where the majority of your stroking work should focus. For example, many dogs could be rated a 1 or 2 when you stroke their heads. They seem to really enjoy it and may even actively seek it. Anything that starts out between 1 and 3 is good to go; you will be able to work with that area of the body fairly easily.

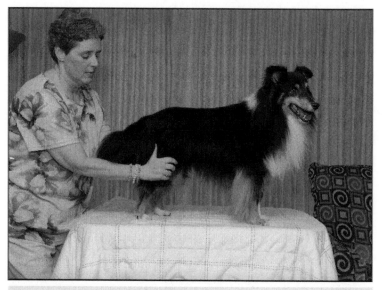

Quest looking comfortable and relaxed while Judy handles his back legs.

However, you will find areas that will be rated as a 4 or 5. A dog can dislike something but still allow it. His body language will make it clear that he's not happy. You may be able to "get it done" but that doesn't change his feelings about what's happening, except maybe to move him from disliking it to hating. Dogs who actively hate certain types of touch may become defensive in an effort to avoid the touch or they may become aggressive in order to make it stop. Remember, if your dog shows any strong reactions or aggression, stop what you are doing and seek qualified professional help.

You may be surprised to find that your dog reacts differently to the body scan than you expect. Often, dogs quickly distinguish between casual, enjoyable touching and handling that has a specific purpose or goal. They become suspicious and uncomfortable when touching suddenly seems to be "all business" rather than just petting.

Your goal is to be able to stroke your dog with very firm pressure while he holds still. Always proceed slowly and gently, and note your dog's reactions to each body area. You will be able to easily add more pressure to those areas where you rated your dog between 1 and 3. Proceed much more carefully with your dog's more sensitive areas (the areas where he is a 4 or 5). Take your time with each individual area as you add pressure. If your dog seems unable to tolerate stroking at the current level, go back to an easier one. Remember, there is no rush. Every successful training session you have brings you closer to your goal.

Pushing

Once your dog is comfortable with being stroked all over his body,

and you have repeated the process in your training place, you can move on to the next handling exercise: pushing. "Pushing" means putting more intense pressure on an area of the dog's body to encourage him to move away. Take a flat hand, place it on your dog's shoulder or hip, and apply steady pressure there. If your dog seems sore or uncomfortable, choose a different area to push.

Your dog will likely resist the pressure at first; that is a normal response. However, your goal is to get your dog to move away from pressure rather than resist it because this is the first step towards being able to manipulate his body and move him into a variety of positions. Apply just enough pressure to get your dog to move away, even slightly. Even leaning away from the pressure is enough. Push lightly, wait for him to move away, use your calm marker, then treat. Over a number of sessions, you should be able to apply more pressure, and your dog should move away from that pressure more easily.

Poking

Poking happens when you apply pressure with the tips of your fingers. A poking type of touch is common in many veterinary exams. Although the dog was encouraged to move away when pushed, the goal of the poking exercise is for the dog to hold still and allow it.

Normally, being poked is an unpleasant event, so it's important to introduce this exercise at a very mild level and increase intensity gradually over a number of sessions. Poke so lightly that you're really just touching your dog with your fingertip, use your calm marker, and treat. Repeat, repeat, repeat in a variety of locations on your dog's body. Very, very slowly increase the amount of pressure you use.

Be cautious of poking too hard in soft or sensitive areas of your dog's body. Watch your dog's response closely; he could have a sore spot or minor injury that makes him react poorly to being poked. If you notice what seems to be an overreaction, you may have found a painful area. Leave it alone for a few days and then check again. If it's still a problem, consult your veterinarian.

Pinching

As with poking, being pinched is a very unpleasant sensation. We don't like it! But pinching will happen to your dog, especially when he gets injections, and you can help him be more comfortable with this reality.

Gently take a bit of your dog's skin from around the shoulder or hip between your thumb and forefinger, pull it slightly away from your dog's body, use your calm marker, and treat. This is referred to as "tenting" the skin to make room for a shot. Over a number of repetitions, you can gradually pull the skin further away from the body. Then you can begin applying more pressure to your grip. You can also increase the amount of time you pinch your dog. Remember to work slowly and only add one new aspect at a time.

Another place to practice this action is on the front of your dog's front legs. There is less loose skin to work with there, but blood is often drawn and IVs are frequently placed in the front leg, so it's an important area to practice with pinching. Blood can also be drawn from the upper part of the back leg, so that is a good place for a little pinching practice as well.

Squeezing

Squeezing refers to applying steady, even pressure on both sides of the body (shoulders or hips), or to a specific body part such as a leg.

To squeeze the shoulders or hips, put one hand on each side, then apply light, equal pressure. Use your calm marker and treat. As long as your dog is comfortable, you can increase the intensity level of the pressure by small amounts over a number of repetitions.

To squeeze the legs, start by wrapping your hand around the leg. Mark and treat your dog for that before you start adding pressure. With each successful repetition, add a bit more intensity to your hold. You are likely to find that some legs will be more sensitive than others. That's fairly normal.

Restraint

Restraint is the next step beyond squeezing. In addition to applying firm, steady pressure, you will also add duration. You will apply enough pressure to keep your dog immobile for a second or two at first, increasing that time as you go along.

Start by restraining your dog in the areas you practiced squeezing.

When he's comfortable with that, move on to holding your dog's head between your hands. Use just enough pressure to keep his head still without hurting him.

You can also restrain your dog by holding him so that the side of his body is up against your chest and your arms are wrapped around his front and back. Practice this from both sides.

In real life situations, there may be times when your dog must be restrained against his will, but in training, your dog should always get a choice. If he becomes uncomfortable, starts to struggle, or panics immediately let him go! Don't fight to keep your hold on him. He's telling you that he's not ready for this step yet, so go back to an easier version of the restraint. Use less pressure and a shorter duration and slowly build your way back up, increasing only one aspect at a time, until your dog can accept the restraint easily.

Lifting
Being lifted off the ground is the ultimate in giving up control. It can be very scary to be lifted far off the ground. Being comfortable with being picked up requires a great deal of trust, time, and experience.

Small dogs naturally get lifted and carried often. Many do not care for it at all in the beginning but adapt over time, while others always hate it. Giant breed dogs rarely get lifted, and when they do, it's usually just the front feet or back feet, and then very briefly. Even so, your giant dog may need to be lifted, likely by multiple people, for a medical exam or emergency. Preparing for that possibility is an excellent plan.

Reaching for and leaning over your dog is the first step to lifting because you can't pick a dog up unless you are very close to him. Spend some time gently invading his space, using your calm marker, and giving him a treat. Move slowly and gradually get closer to your dog in small increments over several repetitions.

Your next step is to begin lifting your dog, just a tiny bit, and for just a second. Just barely move your dog's feet off the floor, use your calm marker while he's elevated, carefully set him back down, and treat. Repeat this while you lift higher and higher. Then go back to a low lift and add a small amount of duration to it. Use your calm marker just before you set your dog down, then give him his treat.
If you have a larger dog, it's easiest to lift only half your dog at a time.

Position yourself in front and slightly off to the side so that you can safely lift your dog's front end just slightly off the ground. Be careful how you grasp and hold your dog for this; you don't want to dig in hard between his ribs or behind his elbows. Keep your palms open and flat against his body. While you lift him, use your calm marker, set him back down carefully, and give him a treat. Do a number of repetitions, lifting just slightly higher each time. Then go back to a very low lift but add a tiny bit of duration to it. Add in more time as your dog becomes comfortable allowing you to hold him in this way. Then repeat with the back half of your dog.

Positions

For both grooming and veterinary care, it is important to move your dog into different physical positions. These positions can be manipulated, meaning that you physically place your dog in the desired position, or they can be taught and put on cue so that your dog moves into position when asked. Both ways are important. There are times when it will be necessary to physically place a dog and times when it's easiest to simply cue your dog.

Stand

Standing is the most basic position used in grooming and vet exams as it allows easy access to all body parts. Standing takes more energy than sitting or lying down, especially for long periods of time, so most dogs will not maintain a stand without a reason. The goal of this exercise is to provide a reason for standing by reinforcing the dog heavily for simply standing still. This is harder than it seems! Many dogs just don't get the concept that standing still and not doing anything is really truly all we want, so you'll need to start out with a very high rate of reinforcement for standing.

The stand position is the start for much of our handling work. We want our dogs to be comfortable holding this position.

The easiest way to establish standing is to lure your dog into standing position and then use rapid fire treats to keep him in that position. Once your treats are gone, you can give your active release cue and toss a treat to encourage your dog to move. Once you have worked on this for a few sessions, you can begin slowing down the rate at which you provide the treats, going from "rapid fire" to "medium fire," and then continuing to slow down treat delivery and morph into the slow treats exercise as long as things are going well.

Once you have established the stand, you can combine it with all the impulse control exercises. This will help your dog maintain his position and keep his focus on the cookies.

Lie Down on the Side

Another common grooming and vet exam position is to have your dog lie on one side. Teaching this position is a continuation of the lifting exercise. The next step is to lift your dog, then tilt forward while still holding him close to your body. Break the tilting forward motion down into small movements, use your calm marker, and set your dog upright

again to give him his treat. The feeling of falling forward is likely to be unsettling to your dog, so take this part slowly and carefully. Make sure you maintain a secure hold as you bend forward so your dog does.

Once you can place your dog on his side on the table, you will need to release him from your grasp and start standing up yourself while he remains still on his side. Be sure to break this down into tiny increments with lots of repetitions.

 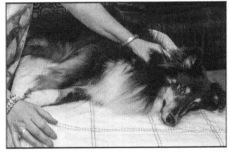

It's also fun to teach your dog to lie down on his side as a trick using luring or shaping. Start by marking and treating your dog for lying down, then for shifting his weight to one hip, then shifting his weight to the shoulder on the same side, and then putting his head down. Break each part of the training down into a large number of repetitions as you go. Don't forget to gradually add duration as well.

Once you've worked on lying down on one side and your dog is comfortable with the process, it's time to work the other side. Repeat the process from the beginning to ensure your dog is comfortable.

Rolling to His Back

It's also likely that there will be times when you need to examine your dog's belly. It's pretty easy to move from lying on the side to rolling to the back. It's just a short way from one to the other! If you gently roll your dog slightly to the side, he should move on to his back.

Some dogs may resist this movement. Being belly up is a pretty vulnerable position, so be sure that your dog is completely comfortable and relaxed on his side before you move to this step. Roll him just an inch or so, use your calm marker, then move him back to his side for a treat. This way, he gets used to the movement before you try to move him all the way to his back.

Once he is on his back it seems like a pretty good idea to give him a belly rub - if he likes that, of course!

Bath Time

Every dog is going to need a bath at some point; some much more often than others. The typical method for giving dogs a bath is to strong arm them into a tub or shower, restrain them there, and do what you have to do as quickly as possible. Even if your dog doesn't mind the water itself, the entire process is likely to end up being relatively unpleasant because it is coerced from start to finish.

There is quite a bit of preparatory training that you can do to make bathing a more pleasant experience for your dog. One very useful side effect of training in this way is that it can also be used to teach dogs to step in a shallow tub of water so you can easily wash off muddy feet.

Start with a low plastic storage container, large enough for your dog to stand in comfortably. For a large dog, an underbed storage container is perfect. You'll also need a bath mat, like one you would use inside your own tub to avoid slipping. Choose a mat that is the appropriate size for your container, or cut it down if necessary. Pick

a mat with suction cups on the bottom so it will grip when slightly wet. For later training, you'll also need a pitcher of lukewarm water available.

Begin your bath training with the bath mat on the floor. Work on this as you did with the mat target by reinforcing your dog for moving towards it and then for being on it. If you've done your mat work well, this process will go very quickly. The main difference between the mat and the bathmat is that we want our dogs to remain standing on the bath mat. Feed your dog in a standing position.

Reward your dog for stepping into the tub, feed him a few treats while he's there, then encourage him to leave by tossing a cookie away.

Once your dog is happily standing on the mat, put the mat inside the plastic container. Then repeat the steps you just followed to teach your dog to stand on the bathmat on the floor. Again, this shouldn't take very long. Continue to mark and treat your dog for staying in the container. About every ten treats, release him with a cookie tossed on the ground.

Once your dog is happily stepping in the container and staying there while you feed him, start adding a tiny bit of water from a pitcher. With your dog out of the container, make sure he sees you add a tiny amount of water, then put the pitcher aside and go back to marking and reinforcing your dog for getting in the container again. You may have to lower your criteria because the addition of water has made the behavior more challenging.

This is a process that is best done slowly and thoughtfully. It is better to take longer to accomplish this than to add too much water too soon and have your dog decide that he doesn't like it. At this point his feet may not even be damp, but that's okay.

As your dog becomes comfortable with getting back in the container, add another tiny bit of water. Repeat this process over a number of training sessions. Pretty soon your dog will be getting soggy feet and he won't care!

You can also start adding some water while your dog stays in the container. Feed with one hand while you pour with the other. As you continue, you can start pouring the water closer and closer to your dog, eventually splashing a bit on him.

Remember, your dog always has the choice to leave if he gets worried or nervous. This tells you that you moved too fast and need to back up and work at an easier level before slowly increasing the challenge level.

At this point you may want to transfer your bath training to the actual tub or shower you'll be using. When you make this change, it's smart to "go back to kindergarten" since the change of location will make things more difficult again.

Final Thoughts on Body Handling

Throughout this step, you are introducing your dog to the types of touch and movement that will be common during grooming or vet visits. The goal is to make these things routine and familiar.

Always keep in mind that the best trainers split everything they teach down into tiny steps. If you are stuck and don't seem to be making any progress, it's likely you need to break it down even further and make it even easier.

Also, remember classical conditioning! Your dog should be feeling pretty good about the whole process. If you see signs of resistance or nervousness, it's time to stop and reconsider your approach. Pushing forward despite your dog's signals that he's not comfortable is never a good plan.

By the time you're done with this step your dog should be happy to be poked, pushed, squeezed, and restrained!

Step 3 checklist for General Body Handling:

Start all exercises on the floor and then move to grooming area when your dog is comfortable:

Handling:

- ❑ Dog is comfortable with stroking all major body parts
- ❑ Dog yields to pushing on shoulder and hip and moves away from pressure
- ❑ Dog tolerates poking on all body parts
- ❑ Dog tolerates pinching on shoulders, hips, front legs, back legs
- ❑ Dog tolerates squeezing of shoulders and hips

Restraint:

- ❑ Dog is comfortable with head restraint
- ❑ Dog is comfortable with shoulder restraint
- ❑ Dog is comfortable restrained by your arms around the front & back of his body
- ❑ Dog allows himself to be gently lifted while restrained

Positions:

- ❑ Dog will maintain a standing position in the grooming area
- ❑ Dog can be physically placed on each side
- ❑ Dog will respond to cues to lie down on each side
- ❑ Dog willingly allows himself to be rolled onto his back
- ❑ Dog responds to cue to roll onto his back

Bathing:

- ❑ Dog will stand on a bath mat on the floor

❑ Dog will stand on a bath mat in a low plastic container

❑ Dog will willingly move into container with a small amount of water in the bottom

❑ Dog will stay in the container while you pour in a small amount of water

❑ Bath mat and container are transferred to tub or shower and process is repeated

Step Four:
Working with the Head

Now that your dog has gotten comfortable with being touched and moved in general, it's time to work on familiarizing him with specific grooming and veterinary tasks. Step 4 will focus on the head because that seems like a logical place to begin. There are quite a few things that may need to be done around the dog's head and face like cleaning out ears, brushing teeth, giving eye drops, and so on.

Chin Rest

The chin rest is an extremely useful behavior to teach for two main reasons. First, it helps your dog learn to hold his head still. This makes it an excellent foundation skill for more specific procedures. Second, because the chin rest is a voluntary behavior, it becomes a very good barometer of your dog's comfort level. Dogs who have learned the chin rest tend to love doing it because they have gotten so much reinforcement. Therefore, if they choose not to do it, it's an excellent indicator that they are not comfortable with what's going on.

The basic chin rest position is for your dog to hold his chin still in the palm of your hand. You should also teach a chin rest to a pillow or towel in your lap, or on a stool or ottoman. This will come in handy if you have a large dog or for handling exercises that require you to have both hands free.

Your dog should be facing you and can be either sitting or standing for this exercise. Begin by gently placing your hand under your dog's chin. Use your calm marker and give your dog a treat. Then repeat over and over.

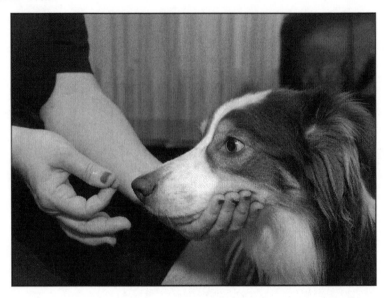

Once your dog is comfortable with that, hold out your hand but don't place it directly under your dog's chin. Hold it about an inch below your dog's head and an inch forward. You want to see your dog move his head towards your hand, even slightly. Mark and treat for even the slightest head movement towards your hand.

Don't hold out for too much here. Remember, training builds everything one tiny step at a time.

Once your dog is regularly placing his head in your hand, you can encourage duration by using your calm marker and feeding in position. It's okay if he moves his head away when he hears the mark; simply provide the treat so that it lures him back into position. Most dogs are pretty quick to figure out that staying in position after the marker is the smart thing to do because the treat is coming to that spot. It's fine if your dog moves away once he gets the treat, but if he stays in position, mark and treat again. Your goal is to get approximately five seconds of duration before you move on to the specific exercises.

There is another very useful variation of this exercise called the double chin rest. For this, rather than placing his muzzle in one of your hands, your dog places it in both your open palms.

Once your dog is comfortable placing his muzzle in both your open hands you can add in yet another variation called the muzzle wrap.

With the muzzle wrap you will move your thumbs up the sides and over the top of your dog's muzzle. This is a very stable position, but can feel quite constraining to your dog. Work first just lifting your thumbs up the sides of the muzzle, marking and treating for that. Eventually you'll be able to move your thumbs over the top of your dog's muzzle and even put a small amount of pressure there.

You do NOT want to add a verbal cue for the chin rest. Instead, the cue is your open palm placed just in front of your dog. Think of it as an invitation that your dog can accept or not. Once trainers add verbal cues to behaviors, things can become more complicated. People often repeat the cue over and over, which means either the dog doesn't truly understand the behavior or that the trainer is putting too much pressure on him to perform the behavior when he is not comfortable.

Ears

Ear care is quite common for many dogs. Some dogs needs their ears flushed and cleaned regularly. Others are prone to ear infections. Many need the hair in and around their ears brushed and trimmed. And of course, checking the ears is always part of a standard veterinary exam.

Ear work starts with stroking. Once your dog is comfortable with that, add in a little gentle squeezing and even pull on them slightly. Move the ears back and forth. Turn an ear inside out so you can look inside. Repeat each action, followed by a mark and treat, as many times as needed to help your dog become comfortable. Remember to break down each action into small movements. If you do something and your dog objects, reinforce anyway, but use a lower level of intensity or smaller motion for the next repetition.

Ear drops are commonly used to keep ears clean or treat infections. Often the drops need to be put in the ear, rubbed around, and the excess wiped out with a cloth or cotton ball. This is a fairly invasive procedure, particularly if your dog's ear is already sore. But, as with everything else, if it is broken down into small steps and practiced regularly, your dog will learn to tolerate it.

Note the use of the pillow chin rest, which frees up both hands to hold Helo's ear and the bottle of drops.

In my Cooperative Care classes, I often see dogs who have a strong negative reaction to even the sight of the bottle of ear drops. If this is the case for your dog, simply set the bottle out while you work on handling his ears. When he can tolerate the sight of the drops, pick up the bottle - but don't move it towards your dog - then mark and treat. Once your dog is good with you picking up the bottle, you can move it a bit closer, mark, and treat. Over many repetitions, you can work towards touching the outside of your dog's ear with the closed bottle. Then work towards touching the inside of your dog's ear with the closed bottle. Take as much time as needed, whether that is several minutes or several months.

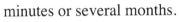

Helo is getting comfortable with the sight and smell of the drops while practicing his chin rest on the pillow.

In separate sessions, you can also work on stroking the inside of your dog's ear with a dry cotton ball. Break this down into the same small steps as described with the bottle. Pick up a cotton ball, mark, and treat. Move cotton ball closer to your dog, mark, and treat. Eventually turn back the ear flap and touch the cotton ball to the inside of the ear, mark, and treat. Break this down into as many small movements as your dog needs to be comfortable and successful.

Once your dog is comfortable with both those things, you can put a few drops of ear cleaning solution on the cotton ball and let your dog sniff it. Mark and treat. Use small steps and several repetitions to move it towards the ear until you can gently wipe the inside of the ear.

While it may seem like quite a bit of training to get to the point of actually using ear drops, the pay off for putting in this foundation work is huge. Your dog will be calm and comfortable, and you won't have to struggle with him to get the drops in!

Eyes

Eye care at the vet's office usually involves holding the head still for an exam while shining a bright light into the dog's eyes. Eye drops are also common both at the vet and at home.

Begin work on your dog's eyes with a chin rest, then peer into your dog's eyes. Sometimes your intense gaze can make your dog uncomfortable, so be sure to mark and treat often. Once your dog is comfortable with this, you can add some duration to gazing into your dog's eyes.

To prepare your dog for the possibility of eye drops, start with an empty dropper (which can be purchased at any drugstore). Introduce the dropper as you did the ear drop bottle. Pick up the dropper, mark, and treat. Move the dropper closer and closer to your dog's face over a number of repetitions.

The next step is to get your dog to accept water drops falling on his muzzle and head. Every time you release a drop of water, your dog gets a mark and treat.

Once your dog is comfortable with you drizzling water drops on his head and face, you can switch to real eye drops. Check with your veterinarian for a recommendation for safe, neutral eye drops. Quickly review the steps you followed with the dropper with the bottle of real drops before you begin putting the drops in his eyes.

Teeth

Dental care is a very important aspect of your dog's health. Being able to open his mouth to examine it, put your fingers in his mouth, and brush his teeth are all very helpful procedures to train.

Your dog's teeth are, of course, the most dangerous part of his body. If he chooses to bite due to fear or stress, someone will get hurt. The goal is to never let it get to that point, so remember, safety is always first. Do not attempt this type of handling on your own if you feel there is any chance you may be bitten.

Handling the dog's muzzle starts on the outside. Start with stroking, then add a bit of pressure, and then move the lips up slightly. Be sure to move slowly and to mark and treat often.

Once you can handle the outside of the muzzle, you can start manipulating the mouth by pulling up on the sides of the lips to see the teeth. Do this in small steps over several sessions until he's comfortable. When he is, manipulate the front of your dog's mouth and encourage him to open it slightly.

Remember, every time you handle your dog's body, you should be marking while your hands are still on your dog, then providing a treat after. If your dog becomes resistant at any point, that is feedback telling you to go back to an easier step and work forward again.

The next step will be actually putting a finger inside your dog's mouth, but on the outside of his teeth. Lift your dog's lip and run your finger over a tooth, then mark and treat. This is easiest to start on the sides and in the front before moving towards the back of his mouth.

As you touch your dog's teeth, you'll find an opening on the sides just behind the canines. Gently insert a finger in your dog's mouth in this opening and move it around a bit until your dog is comfortable. This should cause your dog to relax his mouth and more readily open it. This is great because the ultimate goal is to open the dog's mouth to look inside and to feel around. Take the steps towards this goal very slowly using ample reinforcement along the way.

Brushing your dog's teeth is an extension of the work you've done to this point. Begin by introducing the toothbrush. There are many different brands and types of dog toothbrushes available, but I prefer to use a human child sized toothbrush. At first, simply show it to your dog, mark, and treat. Then move it towards him in increments.

Then touch it to the outside of his mouth. Then put your hands in his mouth while you touch the toothbrush gently to a tooth. Remember, this process should be broken down into as many small steps as possible and you should mark and treat often. As your dog becomes comfortable with the toothbrush in his mouth, you can move it around slowly at first, then more vigorously.

Finally, add some doggie toothpaste (NOT human toothpaste) to the process. Many dog brands seem to taste fairly good, so dogs are generally pretty happy to do this step. I have also done this procedure using baby food before switching to doggie toothpaste. Introduce the toothpaste slowly. 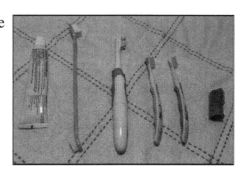 Start by putting some on your finger and letting your dog lick it. Then put your finger covered with toothpaste in your dog's mouth and rub his outside teeth and gums a bit. You can become more vigorous with your rubbing over a number of repetitions. Finally, combine the toothpaste and the toothbrush. When you do this, you'll likely need to go back to simply putting it in your dog's mouth, then moving it just a bit, then more vigorously, and so on. Every time you add something that makes the training harder, it's important to drop back to easier levels with everything else.

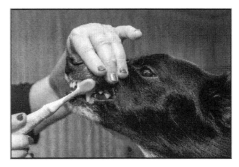

Muzzle Training

Every dog should be trained to comfortably wear a muzzle. You never know when one might be necessary, but it's usually in the midst of a highly stressful situation. If your dog has been prepared for wearing a muzzle, that's one less stressor your dog has to endure.

Sometimes people object to muzzle training because they don't think their dog would bite someone, but keep in mind that any dog has the ability to bite, particularly when scared or in pain. For the safety of everyone involved, a muzzle can be an excellent option. Make it just another one of those bizarre things that your dog tolerates in exchange for food.

There are a variety of different types of muzzles. The proper choice depends on your dog's size and face shape. The two most common types used are basket muzzles and cloth muzzles. It's a good idea to condition your dog to both types because you never know which kind might be available when you need one.

Begin muzzle training the same way you have introduced all equipment so far by showing it to your dog, marking, and treating. After several repetitions of being rewarded for simply looking at the muzzle, hold the muzzle still at an appropriate height and distance for your dog and wait. You want him to move towards it rather than you moving it towards him. The goal is for your dog to

Helo voluntarily putting his face into the muzzle and getting reinforced with squeeze cheese.

voluntarily push his nose into the muzzle. Strive to mark while your dog is moving towards or has his face pushed into the muzzle, then treat.

Once your dog is comfortable with voluntarily putting his nose in the muzzle, you can then purposely move it towards him. It's likely he'll happily meet you halfway. That's perfect!

Spend a handful of sessions working with the straps, keeping them long and not fastening them at first. Simply move them around the back of your dog's head, mark, and treat. Take your time working up to actually buckling the straps. Be aware that the sound of the closure can also be unpleasant for some dogs. This is an important aspect of muzzle wearing that you can isolate.

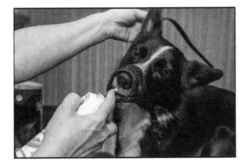 

Before you try snapping the straps together for the first time, spend some time conditioning your dog to the sound of the closure. Hold the muzzle away from your dog, snap it closed, mark, and treat. Do this as you progressively move it closer so that it is eventually behind your dog's head. Then you can snap it shut while he is wearing it.

The initial sensation of having the muzzle firmly attached can lead some dogs to panic. Be prepared to take it off immediately. Don't push for duration wearing the muzzle until your dog is calm having it firmly attached.

Once your dog is calmly wearing the muzzle, it's a good idea to have him move around with it on. Start with very short distances, just a step or two. Work up to him wearing it while moving further distances. The purpose of the movement is to keep your dog's focus off the feel of the muzzle. When first wearing one for any length of time, some dogs may try to rub it off or use their feet to get it off. Movement can keep them from doing that and give them a chance to adjust to the feel.

Taking Medication

Most dogs need to take medications (either in pill or liquid form) at some point in their lives. While some dogs are naturally easy to medicate, others are masters at ferreting out anything they find unusual and treating it as poison. Even for the easy dogs, some medicines taste and/or smell bad, so developing a quick and easy way to administer medicine when it is needed is very useful.

It's not so much about the actual medicine, but rather the procedure surrounding it, that we can work to prepare our dogs for. If we establish a specific pattern and long history of providing tasty things to our dogs in both liquid and solid form, then they will get used to swallowing pretty much anything we offer without suspicion.

For liquids, an empty syringe or plastic dropper can be used as the vehicle for delivery. Mix up something smelly, tasty, and liquidy. For example, take meat-flavored baby food and thin it out with some water. Another option might be some pureed liver - if you can stand the smell! You want a consistency that you can easily suck it up into the syringe or dropper and then dispense. All you need to do is offer this to your dog and allow him to lick it while you slowly release the liquid. Work towards being able to actually place

the syringe in your dog's mouth and then squirting the liquid in. You can vary the liquid that you use, and every once in awhile, simply give some plain water just to mix it up. In order to get your dog used to the possibly bitter taste of certain medications you can add a tiny bit of apple cider vinegar to the contents of the syringe.

Pills can be hidden in a variety of soft smelly foods. We have had great success with a homemade mixture of milk, peanut butter, and flour. Mix 1 part milk, 1 part peanut butter, and 2 parts flour together until it is the consistency of modeling clay and keep it in the fridge. It is sticky enough to coat pills yet very easy to mold.

 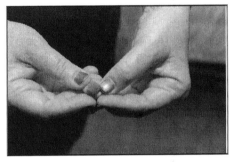

As a pill taking ritual, introduce the three treat procedure. The first is a regular treat, the second contains the pill, and quickly follow with the third regular treat. It's really important to give that third treat as quickly as possible. If your dog is anticipating the next treat he'll swallow the one he has without thinking about it.

Final Thoughts on Working Around Your Dog's Head

It is very normal for your dog to be uncomfortable with someone working around his head and face. It goes against all your dog's natural tendencies to let people handle this part of his body. Just imagine someone suddenly walking up to you, grabbing your face, and sticking his hands in your mouth. You would strongly resist. The same is true for our dogs, which is why this area requires quite a bit of preparation for husbandry care.

People often wonder how long it will take to do this type of work. My answer is always, "It takes as long as it takes." Trying to rush through the tasks only leads to setbacks. Moving forward in a slow and steady manner is what will lead to success.

You are doing your dog a HUGE favor by preparing him for all these different types of handling around his head and face. The more work you put into this preparation, the more relaxed and comfortable you both will be.

Step 4 checklist for Working with the Head:

Chin rest:

- ❑ Chin rest in each hand separately

- ❑ Chin rest on a towel or pillow

- ❑ Chin rest on a chair or stool

- ❑ Double chin rest

- ❑ Double chin rest with muzzle wrap

Ears:

- ❑ Ears stroking

- ❑ Ears squeeze & gentle pull

- ❑ Introduction to ear drop bottle

- ❑ Dog holds still while bottle is moved towards ears

❑ Dog holds still while bottle touches ears

❑ Stroking inside of ears with a cotton ball

❑ Adding ear drops to cotton ball

❑ Stroke inside ears with drops on cotton ball

❑ Place drop into ear and rub lightly

Eyes:

❑ Peer into dog's eyes

❑ Introduce empty dropper and move towards dog's face

❑ Add water to the dropper and drop on head/muzzle

❑ Introduce real eye drops

❑ Drops close to eyes

❑ Drops into eyes

Teeth:

❑ Stroke outside of muzzle

❑ Pull up lips to see the teeth

❑ Insert a finger into mouth and run over outside of teeth

❑ Insert a finger into mouth between teeth

- ❑ Use fingers to gently open your dog's mouth

- ❑ Introduce your dog to a toothbrush

- ❑ Introduce dog toothpaste on your finger

- ❑ Add dog toothpaste to toothbrush

- ❑ Begin brushing movements

Muzzle training:

- ❑ Reinforce your dog for moving towards the muzzle

- ❑ Shape your dog to put his face into the muzzle

- ❑ Practice purposely moving the muzzle towards your dog

- ❑ Move straps around behind your dog's head

- ❑ Condition the sound of buckling the straps while it is away from your dog's head

- ❑ Move the buckling sound closer and closer to your dog

- ❑ Put on the muzzle and buckle it

- ❑ Dog moves a short distance while wearing the muzzle

Medication:

- ❑ Your dog eagerly takes tasty food from a syringe

- ❑ Your dog takes plain water from a syringe

❑ Your dog takes food mixed with a slight bit of apple cider vinegar from a syringe

❑ Your dog happily takes empty pill pockets

❑ Your dog happily takes 3 pill pockets in a row

I took Deb Jones's class with my older great dane Raven after she already disliked getting her nails done and having to undo damage from years of non-cooperative care. Deb's method was systematic and yielded progress that we otherwise would not have seen. I am using Deb's cooperative care method immediately with my new great dane puppy.

~ Tanya Mayer

Step Five:
Foot and Nail Care

Even though I strongly suggested that you start at the beginning of the book and work your way through each step in order, my guess is that many folks opened to this page first. Why? Because this is your most pressing problem! And I get that, but even so, jumping in here won't be all that helpful. You've skipped over some really important stuff. I STRONGLY recommend that you go back and work through the initial steps in order. This is important because if you haven't done the foundation work, trying to pick up at this point is doomed to failure. You simply cannot start in the middle and expect the best outcome. Please go back, take your time with the early work, and you will be in good shape when you get back here again!

Feet

Many dogs are incredibly sensitive to having their feet touched and handled. You've probably discovered that already. You may have also discovered that some feet are less sensitive than others. You may be working at very different levels with different feet.

Think about how you would normally handle your dog's feet as you prepare for trimming hair or nail trims. That handling should be introduced separately before you work with any tools like scissors or clippers. Getting your dog comfortable with you touching, stroking, squeezing, and lifting his feet is important preparation work.

Work one step at a time towards being able to hold a foot, squeeze it a bit, and isolate each toe. Be sure to practice doing this in the position you and your dog will ultimately need to be in for you to be able to trim his nails. Complete each step separately, treating your dog regularly, and taking your time to ensure he is comfortable with having his feet handled. Once this has been well practiced, then it's time to add your tools.

 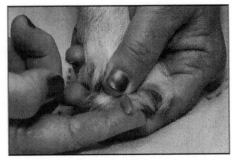

Choosing the Right Tool

The two main ways that people trim their dog's nails is either cutting with clippers or grinding them down with a dremel-type tool. That choice is between you and your dog! Some folks find it is simply easier for them to use one or the other. Sometimes your dog will have a clear preference. You may need to change from one to the other if your dog shows a strong dislike of the one you are currently using. Some people use both tools, using clippers to trim the length and then a grinder to smooth down the edges. In addition, some people find it easier to work with a regular nail file, just like you would with your own nails.

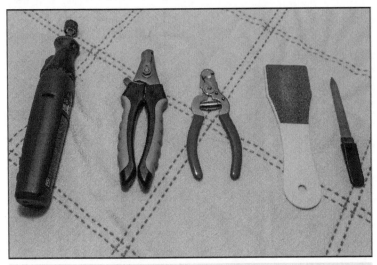

Three tools for keeping nails short: grinder, clippers, and files.

It's impossible for me to give specific recommendations on the tools you should use because there is a huge personal preference factor for this. I like a particular brand of grinder because it's light and fits in my hand well. Someone else might find it too small and not powerful enough. Clippers need to be suited to the size of the dog, but it's also important that clippers are replaced regularly so they are sharp. Dull clippers squeeze too much and can cause discomfort. I don't want to spend too much on something I'll replace regularly, but going too cheap is usually a bad idea too. If you're not sure which specific tool is best suited to your needs, it can be helpful to get recommendations from your friends, particularly those who have dogs that are similar to yours. Also, if you know any professional groomers or handlers, ask them what they use. It will be a matter of trial and error to find the equipment that works best for you.

Introducing Tools to Your Dog

When introducing the clipper or grinder to your dog, go back to pure classical conditioning. Don't ask him to do anything; simply expose him to the tool. Show your dog the tool, mark and give him a treat, briefly move the tool away, then present it again, mark and treat, and so on. Over many repetitions, you can move the clippers closer and closer to your dog. You don't want your dog to interact with the tool at all. Rather, the goal is for him to hold still as it moves toward him.

Next, you want to be able to lightly touch the tool to his foot without him moving away. If your dog moves at first, that's okay. Go ahead and mark and treat your dog, but make your next repetition easier so he's less likely to move. Repeat this procedure for each foot. Remember that each foot is independent. What you can do with one might not be even close to what you can do with another. If your dog becomes resistant at any point, always back off and make it easy enough for him to tolerate, then slowly increase the challenge again.

Please note that with classical conditioning the dog is not expected to do anything specific. You are simply pairing the presentation of the stimulus (grinder or clippers) with the presentation of a treat. You may be wondering why I would recommend adding a marker to this process as the marker typically is used to indicate to the dog that the behavior he is performing is earning reinforcement (operant conditioning). However, in this case, the only expectation is that the dog is exposed to the tool.

Using a marker in these situations is done not because the dog is expected to do anything, but because it's a good way to even more strongly connect the tool with the treat. I think of it as marking MY behavior (presentation of and eventually touching with the tool), not the dog's. The goal is for the dog to simply hold still while all this happens. But even if he doesn't, you should still mark and treat. If the dog is moving, then he's not comfortable with the process, so drop back to an easier level of presentation or interaction. For example, try keeping the tool further away for a handful of repetitions.

Work up to actually touching your dog with the tool over a number of short sessions. If your dog shows any signs of discomfort, back up to an easier level and then start increasing the challenge again.

Now the clippers are touching the nail, but I am not trying to cut yet.

If you are working with a grinder, now is the time to introduce the sound. Actually, the grinder not only has sound, but it will also vibrate when touching your dog's nails. You can prepare your dog for both the sound and the vibration with an electric toothbrush! Buy the cheapest one you can find for this. This is a great way to ease your dog into a pleasant introduction to the grinder, and it's also safer because there is no possibility of your dog getting accidentally nicked by the grinder.

Keep the toothbrush or grinder at a reasonable distance from your dog when you turn it on, using the lowest speed available (if your grinder has variable speeds). Then mark and treat your dog and turn it off. Repeat the process in this order. The sound must always come first. Mark while the sound is going, then treat, then turn off the sound. There should be a short one to two second break before you start the sound again. The sound starts, you mark and treat, then the sound stops. Repeat, repeat, repeat. When your dog is perfectly comfortable with this, you can start moving it closer and closer to him.

With the toothbrush, you can safely touch your dog's feet without any chance of hurting him. With the grinder, you have to be very careful to avoid anything except the nail. It's very easy to get your dog's fur wrapped around the grinder - ask me how I know this! If your dog has long hair on or around his feet, it's best if you trim it short before you attempt using the grinder. Also, I have learned from experience that you can ruin your own manicure in a heartbeat with a nick from the grinder.

When you are ready to actually touch a nail with the grinder, make sure you only do a momentary nick, mark that, and treat. These initial touches should be extremely brief and light. If your grinder has variable speeds start with the lowest possible setting. One of the main mistakes that trainers make is becoming greedy. They start to have a little success and then want to move too fast. Remember, every time you push too far and too fast, you are undoing your previous work. Be the tortoise!

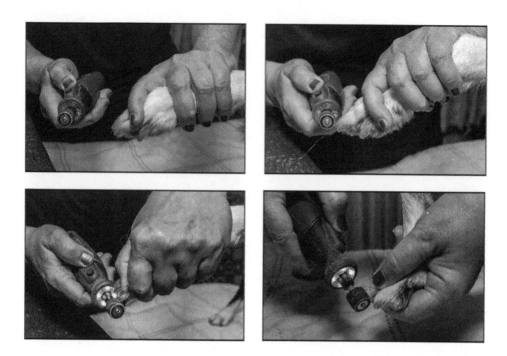

Once your dog is comfortable having one nail touched lightly and briefly with the grinder, you can increase the number of nails you lightly touch with the grinder in a session. Once you are able to do an entire foot, go back to one nail at a time and add a bit more pressure. Repeat the process, working back up to doing an entire foot. This methodical approach is the best way to ensure success.

If you are using clippers, you will first want to be able to tap the top of each nail with the clippers. Then you should work on placing the clippers over the nail, but NOT trying to cut yet. Have patience at this point. Work until you can complete this process with all four feet.

Now the clippers are placed over the nail, but I'm still not trying to cut.

Next, you need to introduce your dog to the sound of the clippers. An easy way to do this is to use them to cut pieces of kibble or other hard food, then allow your dog to eat that food. This associates the sound of something crunching with the presentation of food. Place the clippers close to your dog's feet when you do this.

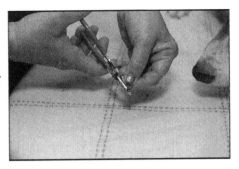

When you are actually ready to clip a nail, remember our mantra that less is more. It is always better to clip a small amount of nail in order to avoid hitting the quick (the vein carrying blood supply to the nail). If your dog has light colored nails, you can see where the quick ends and avoid it, but for dogs with dark colored nails, you simply have to guess.

No matter how careful you might be when clipping your dog's nails, you will cut the quick at some point - probably more than once. It happens. Be prepared by having styptic powder on hand to stop the blood flow because those veins can bleed a lot. If you don't have styptic powder, flour or cornstarch can help. Your dog will likely

yelp when you cut the quick. It's surprising and painful. Your main job in this situation is to remain calm and not freak out. Your dog will remember your reaction so you want it to be no big deal. Give your dog all the cookies you have immediately. Just scatter them in front of him as soon as you can. Then get the blood flow stopped.

The next bit of advice is going to sound wrong to you. You're going to want to ignore it, but please, for your dog's sake, don't. STOP WORKING ON YOUR DOG'S NAILS. Do NOT try to cut any more nails at that moment. Even if you do manage to cut more nails, you will not be ending on success. Rather, you will be in the process of making things worse by continuing to associate fear and pain with having his nails trimmed. If you don't want to completely end the session, switch to something your dog tolerates - or better yet, enjoys - do a few repetitions, then stop. But please believe me when I tell you that leaving the nails alone at this point is the best option.

I follow the 24 hour rule after any traumatic event. It's a good rule for pretty much any unpleasant situation. Simply wait 24 hours before you try another session. Then proceed as if nothing has happened, but drop down to a much easier level and work your way up again. The passage of time without being exposed to the fearful or painful situation means that the event is less likely to be encoded in long-term memory. The old myth that you should return to the same situation as quickly as possible and replace bad memories with good ones doesn't hold true. It's just as likely that you are strengthening the unwanted and unpleasant memories. Returning your dog to the same situation very quickly cements the memory more strongly. Take 24 hours. It can't hurt and it just might help - a lot.

With the grinder you don't usually have to worry about hitting the quick because it is much more gradual and precise. You can round the edges on each side and over the front end of the top of the nail rather than getting too close to the quick in the middle of the nail. This will help the quick recede slowly on its own.

Filing and Self-Filing

Some people choose to use a nail file rather than clippers or a grinder. You can use a hand-held file. There are many different types available at a range of prices. According to my manicurist, glass files are the best quality. While filing your dog's nails will be slower than other methods, you will still be making progress. The handling steps involved in getting to the point where you can hold your dog's foot, isolate a nail, and then file it, will still need to be trained.

© Aleks Woodroff

Other people have decided to go a step further and train their dogs to file their own nails. Self-filing involves a fair bit of training, but it's a fun project to work on. You can make a scratch board with a piece of wood covered with sandpaper. The goal is for your dog to scrape his nails down the board, thereby shortening them on his own.

You will need to teach front foot scratching and back foot scratching separately. Front foot scratching is usually much easier for dogs to learn. Start with your board angled slightly. Mark and treat your dog for touching it with his front feet. You will want to reward more powerful foot movements. When your dog is regularly touching the board, continue to angle it up until is is vertical. This should encourage more of a scratching motion using the nails rather than the entire pad of the paw.

Then there are the back feet to consider. First, you'll want to work on having your dog step on a large flat object on the ground, like a piece of cardboard. Mark and treat whenever your dog's back feet are on the cardboard. I toss the treat forward off the board so my dog pushes off to get the treat. This pushing behavior is the first part of scratching with back feet.

In addition to or instead of a flat scratchboard you may want to consider a curved one. Cutting a piece of PVC lengthwise and then lining the inside with sandpaper gives you a tool that will more evenly shorten all nails rather than mainly the middle two.

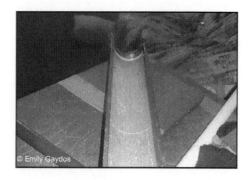

How long should your dog's nails be?

The general rule is that your dog's nails should be short enough that they don't click when he walks on a wood or tile floor. When the nails hit the floor, they put pressure on the nail bed and foot. This is not only uncomfortable, but it also alters your dog's gait, pushing more weight on the back side of the feet and legs.

You must shorten your dog's nails slowly over time. Trying to remove too much will be painful and lead to bleeding from the quick. Taking off small amounts of nail on a regular basis is the best approach.

Final Thoughts on Foot and Nail Care

Many dogs are sensitive about having their feet and nails handled. If they have been forced or have had bad experiences, they can quickly become highly resistant. That leaves owners either neglecting to do necessary care or forcing the issue. Neither option is a good one. Your dog's nails will continue to grow for his entire life, and they require routine maintenance to keep him comfortable and healthy. Time spent working on cooperative care for this part of his body will be time very well spent.

Step 5 checklist for Foot and Nail Care:

- ❑ Can touch and handle all 4 legs

- ❑ Can touch all 4 feet

- ❑ Can pick up all 4 feet

- ❑ Can hold each foot for several seconds

- ❑ Can squeeze each foot slightly

- ❑ Can isolate each nail on each foot

- ❑ Dog has been systematically introduced to tool(s) of choice and is comfortable with them

- ❑ Dog has been introduced to the sound of the grinder and/or clippers

- ❑ Can move tool towards dog while dog holds still

- ❑ Can touch dog's legs with tool

- ❑ Can touch dog's feet with tool

*Note that you will need to do the following for all nails:

- ❑ Can touch nail with tool

- ❑ Can tap on nail with tool

- ❑ Can clip, grind, or file tiny amount of nail

❑   Can clip, grind, or file tiny amount on all nails

Scratch boards (optional):

❑   Introduction to scratch board for front feet

❑   Introduction to scratch board for back feet

Step Six:
Tools

We've already discussed introducing some basic tools to your training. This section will expand on that topic, including tools for medical exams and grooming.

Playing Doctor

Most of us have grooming tools, but not the tools used by the vet. My favorite way to introduce a dog to a variety of tools that might be used for a veterinary visit is to buy a child's play doctor or play veterinarian kit. These kits come with a wide array of plastic tools, such as a syringe, scissors, scalpel, tweezers, otoscope, and other assorted medical type devices. My kit even came with a pair of fake glasses and a tiny cell phone! While I haven't figured out what to do with the phone yet, getting your dog used to wearing glasses might actually be useful. If he ever needs laser treatments or eye care, some sort of eye protection may be necessary. Even if he never needs such treatment, he will probably look pretty cute in those glasses anyway!

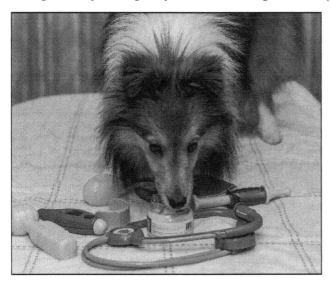

Tigger enjoying baby food while being exposed to the tools in the play doctor kit.

The goal is to introduce a wide variety of tools to your dog. As always, introduce one tool at a time. First mark and treat your dog just for seeing the tool. Then mark and treat for holding still while you move the tool closer and closer, until you can actually touch him with it. You may find that your dog reacts differently when you

touch the tool to different parts of his body. For example, he may be more sensitive when you touch his back end than he is when you touch the front.

Once you can touch your dog with a tool, combine it with some of your earlier handling. For example, pull up some skin on the back of his neck to give him a pretend injection by poking him a bit with the fake syringe. Or use the otoscope to "look" in his eyes or ears. Run the scalpel down a shoulder or poke him lightly with the scissors. The larger variety of actions you can perform with your tools, the better. You want your dog to get to the point where he is so used to this kind of handling that it is simply no big deal. He will have such a huge history of being rewarded for the strange stuff you do to him that he looks forward to it.

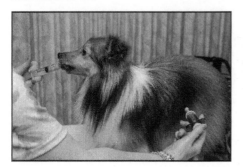

Beauty School

It's likely that you already have a variety of grooming tools like brushes, clippers, scissors, and so on. It's also likely that you've already been using these tools on your dog. It can't hurt, though, to go back a few steps and work on making the appearance and use of these tools a more positive experience. Marking and treating your dog when the grooming tools come out is a great start so that your dog looks forward to seeing the tools. The appearance of the grooming tools should come to mean that lots of treats will now be available.

What if your dog runs away when the grooming tools come out? This happens because your dog has learned to connect the tools with an unpleasant event. You will need to work hard to change this association. The first step is to simply set out one of the tools in a place that your dog passes by regularly. Put a container with treats there as well. Whenever your dog walks past the tool, go ahead and give him a cookie. This cookie is free. Don't ask him to do anything for it. The cookie comes because your dog was close to the dreaded tool. If you do this regularly, it will make an emotional difference to your dog.

The next step is to casually pick up the tool, then toss your dog a cookie. Take this slowly. Don't show your dog the tool by waving it in his face. Instead, just pick it up, give your dog a cookie, and put it down. You can progress to picking it up, carrying it around with you for a bit, giving your dog a cookie, then setting it down. All you're doing here is randomly carrying around the tool. But when you do that, it becomes a signal to your dog that a cookie will soon be available. This transforms something that caused your dog to have an unpleasant reaction into something that now signals a good event. Do this separately with each tool that had an existing unpleasant association.

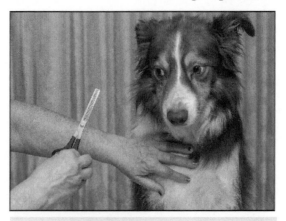

Zen demonstrating his concern about, and dislike of, the scissors.

Even if your dog doesn't already have an unpleasant association with a tool, it can never hurt to go through these early conditioning steps to be sure he develops a positive response. Making grooming tools a regular part of the environment so they are no big deal is a good start. Continuing on this path and making grooming tools a signal for the opportunity to get a treat is even better. Once that is accomplished, you can purposely introduce the tools into husbandry training.

I'll use the example of scissors to discuss the basic process for introducing a tool to your dog.

Start with the scissors sitting in your grooming area. Invite your dog to the area and give him some treats just for being there.

Next, pick up the scissors, give a few treats, and set them down. Repeat this about ten times.

Then pick up the scissors, move them slightly towards your dog, then give him a treat. Repeat this step about ten times. Your dog should be standing still as you move the scissors towards him (being careful with the sharp tips of course).

Continue until you can hold the scissors flat against your dog's body and he is comfortable holding still while that happens.

Now go back to holding the scissors at a distance. Open and close them so they make noise. Treat your dog. Repeat until your dog does not react to the sound.

Move the scissors closer, opening and closing them. Be sure to monitor your dog's reaction carefully. Mark and treat generously through this process.

Now you're at the point where you can trim a bit of hair. But be aware that your dog may tolerate trimming better on certain body parts and not so well on others. Keep a note of his more sensitive areas and focus more work there.

Introducing any tool to your dog should follow this same general sequence. After you have introduced a handful of tools in this manner, it is likely that your dog will begin to generalize the concept that new things lead to high levels of reward. At that point you will probably find that you can speed up your training.

There's No Shame in the Cone!

A cone, sometimes referred to as an elizabethan collar, is a device designed to keep your dog from being able to chew on parts of his body. Cones are used to protect sensitive areas and allow wounds to heal properly. We can't explain to our dogs that they should leave their wounds or surgical sites alone so they can heal. Our only option is to prevent them from causing further damage.

As with a muzzle, all dogs should be taught to comfortably wear a cone. You never know when it will be necessary, and introducing it when your dog is already upset, sick, and in pain is only making a bad situation worse. Spend a little time being proactive about this training and it might make a future bad situation slightly better. Cones come in a variety of materials and designs. You may need to experiment to find the type that works best for you and your dog.

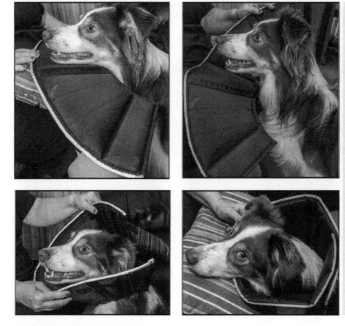

These photos demonstrate the steps you would take to gradually accustom your dog to wearing a cone starting with it wide open on a pillow in your lap. Reinforce your dog highly at each step of the process and move ahead as he becomes comfortable at the current level.

Note: in these photos I am using a sturdy fabric cone.

If you've already taught a chin rest on a pillow, then adding in an open cone to this work will be very easy.

Another approach would be to target train your dog to stick his head into the opening of a closed cone.

Teaching your dog to comfortably wear the cone involves two steps. First, there is getting the cone on. Then increasing the amount of time your dog wears the cone. Once your dog will happily put on the cone, keep him busy while it stays on. The slow treats exercise is an excellent way to build duration by keeping your dog's thoughts occupied by the treats rather than on the feeling of the cone.

In these photos we are using a closed plastic cone. Tigger is being reinforced using a baby food syringe for sticking his head into the cone further and further, until it is all the way on. As always, take this process slowly over a number of short sessions.

Final Thoughts on Tools

Be aware of your dog's reactions and alter your training plan accordingly. By now you should be quite sensitive to even the slightest changes in your dog's emotional state and body language. Always listen to what your dog is saying. Signs of discomfort mean that you are moving too fast or pushing too hard. It never hurts to go back to the place where your dog is comfortable and work a few more sessions there before moving ahead again.

Step 6 checklist for Tools:

Your dog has been introduced to a variety of husbandry and grooming tools and is comfortable with them.

❑   Tools include, but are not limited to:

- ○ Brushes
- ○ Combs
- ○ Scissors
- ○ Spray bottles
- ○ Dryers
- ○ Syringes
- ○ Tweezers
- ○ Otoscope
- ○ Scalpel
- ○ Stethoscope

❑   You can use the tools to stroke, push, and poke your dog in different areas of his body

❑   Your dog has been introduced to the cone (elizabethan collar)

❑   Your dog is comfortable with the cone attached

❑   Your dog is willingly moving around with the cone on

I have found the work we did in our Cooperative Care class to simply be the most useful training I've ever done with my dogs. It has made everyday handling and grooming less stressful for all, and has made the emergencies I have had to deal with much more manageable. Knowing that my dogs can calmly accept being muzzled and handled by veterinarians in a crisis helps me remain calm as well. I recommend this class to everyone who owns a dog.

~ Pattie Boy

Step Seven:
People and Places

Once you've established solid husbandry procedures at home by yourself, it's time to take the show on the road. This is the step where you involve other people and places in your training to ensure that your dog is comfortable with being handled in a variety of places by a variety of people.

Introducing People

Just having another person close by can be challenging for some dogs. This might happen because your dog is a social butterfly and he is doing his best to convince the person to interact with him, or it could be that your dog is tense and nervous with someone else close to him. In either case, adding another person to your training session is challenging.

A good helper can be a huge benefit to your husbandry training. A good helper is someone who listens carefully to your instructions and responds quickly and appropriately. Sometimes a spouse is NOT the best choice for this task!

Bystanders

The helper should start out as a bystander, which is simply a neutral and somewhat disinterested person. The bystander's job is just that: to stand by. The bystander does not interact with the dog in any way - no talking, no touching, no eye contact. The most important variable for the bystander is distance from your dog. Start out with the bystander far enough away so that your dog is aware of the person, but doesn't have a strong reaction of any kind.

Practice your basic husbandry work while the bystander is in the area. If your dog responds as he normally does, then you can ask the bystander to move closer. As you progress, you will find a distance where your dog's behavior changes. He's giving you really important information there. Have the bystander move a few steps away while you work, then a step closer, then another, as long as your dog is comfortable. It really helps if the bystander moves laterally with her side facing your dog. The goal is to have the bystander become meaningless to your dog.

Friendly Strangers

At the groomer and in the vet's office, friendly strangers will be directly interacting with your dog. Typically these are nice folks who like dogs. Even so, that doesn't mean your dog is going to feel positively about the experience, especially if your dog is tense or nervous. Dogs can quickly come to associate the people in these settings with fear and pain. This is why it's important to help your dog learn to tolerate a friendly stranger approaching, greeting, and touching him.

Of course, we are going to break this process down instead of simply allowing a person to come up to your dog. Have your helper stand at a distance and simply turn to face your dog. Mark and treat your dog until he's comfortable and staying still. Then have your helper take one step towards him, then two, and so on. All of this should be done with your helper being neutral (no talking or eye contact yet). We are splitting the approach out from the other aspects of the experience.

During this process, it's fine - even desirable - for your dog to look at the person. Someone sneaking up on your dog would be startling and unpleasant. Be sure to keep your rate of reinforcement high enough that your dog stays still while the person approaches. However, if your dog significantly moves towards or away from the helper, you are likely not reinforcing often enough. Carefully assess why your dog is moving; if your dog is afraid of people approaching, you need to go way back in your training and spend much more time with someone at a distance. If your dog is truly uncomfortable with people approaching, this process will take much longer. There's no rush! Remember, slow progress is better than no progress. Work at the level where your dog is comfortable, never beyond that.

Once your dog is comfortable with the helper approaching, you can add in a greeting. The greeting involves both making eye contact and speaking to your dog. As you can probably guess by now, the best approach would be to split these two components and train one at a time. Start with eye contact. When you introduce eye contact, increase your helper's distance from your dog again. Eye contact doesn't mean a hard stare! That would be intimidating. But it does mean that the helper is looking more directly at your dog as he approaches now. It's okay to smile as well! Follow the sequence of training described above for decreasing distance. You want to be rewarding your dog at a fairly high rate throughout this process.

Once the friendly stranger can approach your dog while making eye contact, it's time to add in a verbal greeting. People love to talk to dogs! And many dogs love it when people talk to them! But we still want to train our dogs for this possibility because very sociable dogs can lose their minds when people talk to them. Their arousal levels increase greatly, causing them to lose any semblance of impulse control. This is better than the opposite issue, where dogs become fearful and anxious when people approach, but it is still a problem for conducting a veterinary exam or for grooming. We need dogs to hold still in these situations. This is where the foundation work we did much earlier will be very helpful. We are going to continue reinforcing for stillness as we add the challenge of a person moving closer, looking at, talking to, and eventually touching and handling your dog.

Ask your helper to talk to you about the dog as she approaches, rather than talking to the dog. The helper can talk to you about how wonderful and well-behaved your dog is as you highly reinforce your dog for holding still. As you continue this work, your helper can add in a bit of talk addressed to your dog as well. Silly zen

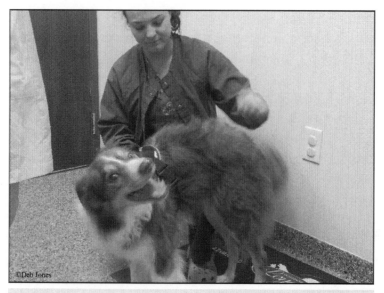

Dogs like Zen naturally enjoy attention and touch from strangers, but not all dogs will.

The next aspect of the friendly stranger approach is for the stranger to actually touch your dog. Your dog will need to be comfortable and calm with a person approaching, making eye contact, and talking to him first. Then you can add in a touch, which should be light and brief at first. You can build up the amount of pressure and the duration of the touch over a number of training sessions.

Introducing Places

Other than your home, the two main places husbandry is likely to take place are at the veterinary office and the grooming shop. The goal is to make these places as pleasant and enjoyable as possible. You don't have to wait until your foundation work is complete to take it on the road. It's a very good idea to visit these locations early and often.

Happy Vet Visits

It's smart to plan your puppy's visits to the vet carefully. You want those first experiences to be very good ones. Of course, choosing a veterinarian whose staff is caring and thoughtful about how they handle their patients is very important. These days many veterinarians are more aware of the value of low stress and gentle handling in their offices and during procedures. Owners are becoming educated about this issue and now actively search out veterinary practices that focus on making the entire experience easier for everyone involved. Don't be afraid to voice your concerns and desires regarding the way your pet is handled.

Many vets are also now open to the idea of "well vet visits." For these visits, you are simply conditioning your dog to learn that the vet's office is a fun place to be. There are lots of tasty treats and nice people. Your pup can get used to the waiting room, the exam room, and some common procedures such as being weighed. Take lots and lots of small, soft, high value treats and be ridiculously generous in treating your dog for simply being there.

*Star and Tigger spending time in the exam room,
relaxing and getting cookies.*

It's very helpful to develop a strong relationship with your veterinarian, as well as the technicians and other staff. This will take time and effort on your part, but it is definitely worthwhile. Share your concerns about husbandry and your training plans with those who will be working with your dog. Most involved will be happy to be helpful because it will make their jobs easier. Show off the results of your work so far! And always encourage the staff to freely feed your dog lots of cookies - be sure to bring extras and have them handy!

If your dog has strong negative associations with the vet's office or staff already, you'll need to control the situation more closely. Don't be afraid to give specific instructions (nicely, of course) on how you'd like people to interact with your dog. Don't be afraid to quickly move your dog out of a situation if he becomes uncomfortable. Your job is to monitor his emotional comfort; take it seriously.

There is more value in short, frequent visits than in less common but longer ones. The value is in the repetition of good experiences. You can go into the waiting room, feed some cookies, leave, take a couple minute break, and repeat over and over.

Zen showing off his tricks for the vet!

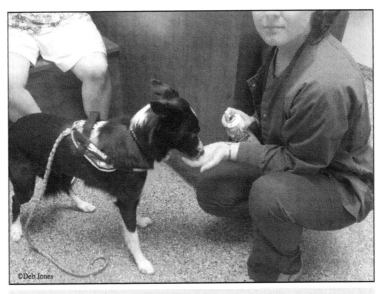

Star is suspicious of strangers and needs to approach them on her own terms in order to become comfortable. This vet tech was willing to get down on the ground, avoid eye contact with Star, and spread squeeze cheese on her hand for Star to lick.

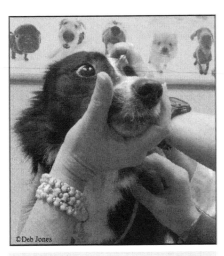

With lots of work on handling first with familiar people and then with strangers, Star is now able to tolerate multiple hands on her at a time.

Of course, no matter how much you try to prepare, there will come a day when something unpleasant or scary happens to your dog at the vet. If you've prepared with lots of happy vet visits, as well as working your foundation husbandry at home, your dog has a good chance of making a quick emotional recovery from the unpleasant experience. Get right back to all your positive conditioning and training again. Bad experiences will set you back a bit, but they won't ruin all your progress as long as you continue working.

What if you have a dog who already has a really bad association with the vet? Then you have more work to do to change his mind. The techniques presented in this book are the same ones you will use, but you will likely need to do many more repetitions at the lower levels to establish comfort and relaxation before you can move forward. It may seem like a daunting task - and it is! - but the time and effort will be worthwhile for your dog's emotional, mental, and physical well-being. Our general rule for husbandry training (actually for all training) is to work at the level where your dog can be successful. That might mean dozens of visits to the vet where nothing happens except lots of cookies.

Getting free cheese from the vet!

Beauty Shop Visits

If your dog will be visiting the groomer, you'll want to help him become comfortable there as well. Grooming shops are often noisy and busy places. There may be many dogs and multiple people working on them. Be very cautious about choosing a groomer. They are not all thoughtful or gentle with the dogs in their care. An experienced groomer who truly loves dogs and treats them well is worth the search.

Treat the grooming shop like the veterinarian's office. Make visits before anything needs to be done. Feed lots of cookies. Expose your dog to all the sights, sounds, and smells of the place. Hang out for a while and let your dog explore as much as possible. Put him on the table and feed him. Show the groomer what you've been working on for husbandry.

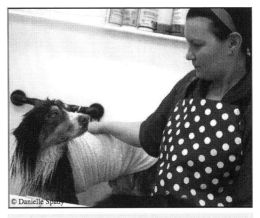

Jessica and Joey.

Final Thoughts on People and Places

For both the veterinarian and the groomer, it's very important to pay attention to your gut feeling about the people and the place, and to watch your dog's reactions carefully. What's the overall mood of the dogs and people? If you can sense stress and anxiety in the environment, then so can your dog. Don't try to talk yourself out of your gut feelings; trust yourself and listen to them. Keep looking until you find a place where you and your dog are truly comfortable.

Think for a minute about how different this training approach is from what typically happens at a vet or grooming visit. If you haven't prepared your dog with husbandry work, things may or may not go well. You go in and people directly approach and talk to your dog, and may immediately begin touching and examining him. If he resists, he will be restrained. If he becomes afraid and can't escape, his next option would be to growl, snap, and bite. It's true that many dogs are fine with this rather thoughtless approach; but you're taking a huge gamble. Anything you can do to prepare ahead of time and make this whole experience better is a huge favor to your dog.

Step 7 checklist for People and Places:

- ❏ Your dog can work on husbandry in a familiar location with a neutral bystander at a distance

- ❏ Your dog can work on husbandry in a familiar location with a neutral bystander moving closer

- ❏ Your dog can work on husbandry in an unfamiliar location with a neutral bystander first at a distance, then closer

- ❏ Your dog can work on husbandry in a familiar location with a friendly stranger in the area

- ❏ Your dog can work on husbandry in a familiar location with a friendly stranger close to him

- ❏ Your dog can work on husbandry in a familiar location with a friendly stranger talking to him

- ❏ Your dog can work on husbandry in a familiar location with a friendly stranger making direct contact with him

- ❏ Your dog is comfortable with the 4 steps above in an unfamiliar location

- ❏ Through many well pet social visits you have established the veterinarian's office as a very good place to be.

- ❏ Your dog is comfortable with the people in your veterinarian's office

- ❏ Your dog is comfortable being touched by people in your veterinarian's office

❑ Your dog is willing to show off his husbandry training in your veterinarian's office!

❑ Repeat the 4 steps above at the grooming shop

❑ Continue maintenance at the veterinarian's office and grooming shop for the rest of your dog's life!

Final Thoughts about Husbandry Training

When is your husbandry training finished? NEVER! It is a lifelong process. My goal is to establish a bank account for husbandry with my dog, and I encourage you to do the same. Make as many "deposits" as you can by establishing a huge reinforcement history for husbandry procedures. Clearly, it is best to start this training early and to keep working on it regularly, whether you see an immediate need or not. Husbandry training is like a retirement fund because it is an investment in the future.

Over your dog's lifetime, you will be making regular withdrawals from the bank of goodwill and tolerance that you have established. Some will be small and negligible, like regular brushing. Others, such as painful emergency veterinary procedures, may cause the bank account to drop to extremely low levels. If you don't replenish your account regularly, you will end up being overdrawn.

That's okay though, because now you know how to build your account back up again. Get back to husbandry training as soon as possible! Keep your bank balance high throughout your dog's lifetime so you and your dog are always prepared for the unexpected.

Please know that there will be regression as a natural part of the learning process. This is particularly likely if you've lightened up on your husbandry training because everything has been fine. Short and regular maintenance sessions will keep most everything on track. The longer the time between training sessions, the more likely regression will occur. Don't be distressed and give up! Just get back to work. You are not back where you started. You are always ahead because of your training. You just can't rest on your laurels and become complacent. Husbandry is a constant work in progress.

What if you never have to use some of the things you've trained for? Well, then both you and your dog are very lucky! But your work still hasn't been wasted. You've spent quality time interacting with your dog. You've worked to make something that might be scary more tolerable or even pleasant. Your dog has learned to trust you more. Your dog will develop more confidence and feel more secure. You've become a better trainer. Your groomer and veterinarian will look forward to seeing you and your dog. All those benefits are there whether  or not you ever need to use any particular procedure you've trained. Husbandry training is one of the most important things you can do for a beloved companion. It's a win-win for both you and your dog.

The idea that my anxious dog might agree to being handled was new to me when I took Deb Jones's class. I no longer dread nail trims or vet visits.

~ Megan O'Connor

I took the cooperative care class with my elderly cat Suki. She had been diagnosed with kidney failure, a disease that is largely managed by supportive care. Through the class she learned to be calm and accepting of fluid injections, medication administration, and blood pressure testing. Learning these behaviors before they were needed greatly enhanced her quality of life and reduced stress as her disease progressed.

~ Deb VE

I took the Cooperative Care with Deb Jones and it has been truly helpful for my dog in veterinary visits and at home as well. My dog has been previously anxious with vets and it helped me to help him be more comfortable.

~ Zane Brown

Cooperative Care: Case Study Reviews

At the beginning of this book I presented a handful of real life case studies of dogs who have serious issues with handling and husbandry. Let's revisit those cases now and take a second look. In addition to the basic case information presented earlier, I'm adding in further information from the owners about what they have tried so far and whether anything has helped. Then I'll say a little bit about what I would suggest.

As you look over these cases after you've read the book, you will probably have some very good ideas about the approaches that would help in each case. If so, then I've done my job here well! Remember also, that there is no one right way. The right way is the one that works for you and your dog without conflict or pressure. You may have to try many options until you find the one, or the combination, that works in any particular case.

Please keep in mind that we have limited information in all of these cases. Recommendations often change when we learn more details. This section is simply meant to give you some general ideas on my thought process and approach to problem solving.

Case #1: Bodhi, German Shepherd Dog, 3 ½ years old

When did you first realize you had an issue with husbandry?

He appeared to have an ear infection and is the only dog ever to not let me put medication in his ear.

What, exactly, did you first notice?

The medication didn't hurt him because it never got near him. He noticed me getting the medicine and somehow figured this was for him and no way no how was he going to let me put something in his sore ear. He ran and hid under my desk. Another time I tried straddling him and he bucked me off. He will let me give him oral medications no problem, but no one is going near that left ear.

What did you do to try to deal with the issue?

I tried feeding his meals one kibble at a time touching his neck, then closer to the ear until I could finally touch the inside of the top of his ear with my fingers. Any lower and he would yelp and run and hide. I tried a squirt gun, maybe a few drops got in his ear, then he was especially suspicious after that.

Is it fixed, better, or ongoing?

Ongoing, we are doing muzzle training. The one kibble at a time method worked the best so far. We will continue to follow the steps from the Cooperative Care class. When I asked about it during your Cookie Pushers session (Facebook Live broadcast) with Denise Fenzi you said when you are dealing with pain you are not starting at zero, but below zero.

I am hopeful we can resolve this if I go especially slow and do not rush things. He is deeply bonded with me and I want to build trust which can be so easily lost with him.

Recommendations:

It's perfectly normal for a dog to 'guard' a painful body part, totally understandable. However, there is a lot we can do in this situation to make things better for Bodhi.

I'd suggest establishing a chin rest on a pillow in your lap as a strong, highly reinforced behavior. This positioning allows you to have both hands free, which will be necessary to eventually place ear drops. Spend plenty of time making this position very valuable to him.

Once you have a strong chin rest to pillow established then you can begin moving your hands around his head, but not touching. Move hand, mark & treat. Repeat, repeat, repeat.

You would work towards touching his muzzle, head, and ears, but very slowly and gently. If he moves away that means you went too fast.

Separately from this I'd work on the appearance of the ear drops predicting cookies. It sounds like Bodhi has learned that ear drops ---> unpleasant things. We want to counter condition that response. So lots and lots of picking up the bottle and tossing him treats long before you ever try to move it towards him. Just have the bottle out in a place you commonly pass by along with a container of treats. Walk by, pick up bottle, toss a cookie, put down bottle.

When you can touch his muzzle, head, and ears then add the ear drop bottle to your sessions. Just have it there, pick it up, mark & treat, put it down. You would start with simply showing him you have it until he's very comfortable. Then, over a series of short sessions, move it towards him.

A cotton ball or ear wipe might be something else to introduce and condition as well. The key is to do all these things separately and at Bodhi's pace. His ability to maintain his chin rest is his way of giving consent for you to continue. If he moves away he's telling you that you moved too quickly.

This is a very fixable situation. Once Bodhi realizes that you are moving at his pace and that there is a huge rate of reinforcement for cooperating with you, he will become more confident and comfortable. Also, respecting his indicators that he is uncomfortable (moving from his chin rest position) and adjusting your training accordingly, will go a long way to making this situation better.

Case #2: Moses, Rhodesian Ridgeback, 1 year old

When did you first realize you had an issue with husbandry?

Around 10 weeks of age.

What, exactly, did you first notice?

Unfortunately Moses had an allergic reaction to a vaccine he received the day before we brought him home and so we had to give him liquid benadryl at the instruction of our vet. He did NOT like this and I think it set us up for a rough road of husbandry. Pretty much right away he didn't like us handling his head, and I think it goes back to that benadryl on day one of being in our house. Thankfully we have been successful with husbandry regarding feet, but anything with the head is a no go. Of course, I tried to do all the things they tell you to do with a puppy: check the ears, check teeth and gums, etc... but I could tell these caused him distress. He would jerk his head away and create distance between us, so I stopped working on it altogether because I didn't want to create more stress around handling with a young pup.

What did you do to try to deal with the issue?

Months ago I started working a chin rest on a towel in my lap. We made some good progress, but I wasn't sure how to move from chin in lap to handling his face. We also are getting a very nice chin rest in my hand and I've started to move my hand toward his face and even gently touch his snout, mark and reward. He is doing well with this and isn't showing stress. I don't know how to approach handling his ears. This is by far the most distressing thing for him.

Is it fixed, better, or ongoing?

Ongoing. I'm not sure how to go from chin rest to actual handling, ESPECIALLY for his ears. Right now he has a scab on his ear from playing with his sister. I'd really like to put some gel on it, but I know he won't let me without a fight and I'm not going that route.

Recommendations:

It's amazing how a single bad experience, especially early in life, can carry such weight for years and years! If only we could counter condition that quickly, but it doesn't work like that.

You are definitely on the right track with the chin rest to a towel or pillow on your lap. This allows you to use both hands for handling work. Make your chin rest as strong and solid as you possibly can. Do LOTS of short sessions with LOTS of reinforcement for holding the position. We want to make that his default consent signal. As long as he holds the chin rest then he's good with what you're doing. If he cannot hold it, then you need to adjust and make things easier for him.

I addressed ear handling in the previous Case Study with Bodhi and my recommendations there apply here as well.

In addition to a chin rest on your lap I'd also suggest teaching a double chin rest in both hands. You can add the muzzle wrap to this over time to steady his head in your hands. This is the beginning of head restraint. However, this is an operant behavior as Moses is choosing to put his head in your hands and keep it there. By making this choice he will feel more comfortable and confident.

In addition, I think you may want to also work on getting Moses to tolerate restraint of his head (separately from the chin rest) in a more passive manner. First condition him that hands moving towards his head predict reinforcement. Reach forward and give him a cookie. Do this often. Then work towards touching him very briefly and giving a cookie. Eventually you would like to place a hand along side of his head. And the ultimate goal is holding his head between both hands. Use liberal treats throughout this process.

And finally, you may want to review the section of the book on giving medications. It's very likely you will need to give liquid or pill form medications, so better to prepare and practice now so you don't have to fight over it later. Start with baby food in a syringe and go from there.

Case #3: Maddie, Mastiff/Boxer mix, 7 years old

When did you first realize you had an issue with husbandry?

In hindsight, she made it clear she did not want strangers taking her temperature rectally from the very first vet appointment I took her to, a few weeks after adopting her. I knew nothing about dogs or behavior at the time, and it didn't seem like a big deal when, after taking her in the back, they reported that "she didn't like the thermometer and tried to alligator roll to get away."

After almost a year (and several more similarly unpleasant vet experiences), she needed a blood draw. The techs had to bring her back out to me to muzzle her, and she continued to thrash around trying to escape the whole time. That was the first time I really witnessed how upset she was, and I started seriously looking into solutions then.

What, exactly, did you first notice?

Over several months, it became clear that she wasn't comfortable with overly interactive strangers in general, and her reactions escalated at unpleasant vet appointments.

She has zero personal space bubble with people she trusts, and doesn't mind being loomed over, paw handling, nail trimming, rear-end wiping, or even blood draws from "her" people. I continue to feed high value treats after any of that to maintain her cooperation.

Basically, her attitude is that her trusted human friends can do pretty much anything to her, and strangers who want to interact are by default a threat.

What did you do to try to deal with the issue?

-Advocating for my dog! Pushing to stay with her as much as possible during vet appointments, and explaining her issues ahead of time and again to each new person we encounter.

-Requesting that they not take a rectal temperature unless absolutely necessary!

-Having vet staff feed her (ideally throwing food on the ground for her so she's not magnetized closer than comfortable)

-Muzzle training (both basket and soft cloth one)

-Holding a peanut butter kong for her to lick (while wearing soft muzzle) during hands-on procedures

-Trazodone ahead of time
-Doing blood draws myself at home

-Asking for vet staff to be in the room when we enter, rather than coming in after us

-Finding a Fear Free regular vet, and visiting just to hang out and have delicious snacks several times before an actual exam (with our vet and tech present - not just at the office, since she's always happy to go in, it's strictly the people that are scary).

-Requesting the same staff at each appointment rather than a new set of strangers each time

Is it fixed, better, or ongoing?

Better, but definitely still ongoing. Emergency and specialist appointments are still tough.

I think everything listed above helps in some way, though often not all of my preferred tools are feasible (like if she needs to be fasted, or they insist on taking her away from me). Bringing my own muzzle (and Maddie happily shoving her face into it) seems to have the added benefit of giving me more credibility with vet staff. The peanut butter kong + soft muzzle alone have gotten us through some pretty invasive orthopedic exams.

Recommendations:

You've already taken a lot of the steps I would recommend with Maddie. Excellent start! Because your issues are specific to the location of exam room, or back of the veterinarian's office I'd spend as much time as possible making that a very good place to be, both alone and with staff present.

Finding a vet educated in cooperative care is the biggest step. Since our vets have taken the certification course they have changed their procedures quite a bit, and all for the better. Our animals are more comfortable, and so are we. Working with unknown bystanders and friendly strangers as suggested in the book should be a big benefit to you. It sounds like the issue with strangers is a fairly strong one that would benefit from being directly addressed without the added stressor of veterinary procedures. Splitting out the people part of the issue from the husbandry part is very important.

You mentioned having vet staff feed her and having them throw food on the ground. This is a good idea. The pressure of moving close to someone she isn't comfortable with in order to get food is going to introduce stress and conflict, which are not desirable. Much better if they ignore her when she approaches and then toss food away for her to get.

Another approach is shown in one of the pictures in the last section of this book. You can see Star with a vet tech. The tech is squatting down, looking away from Star, and has put squeeze cheese on her hand for Star to lick. She is NOT looking at her, talking to her, or encouraging her to approach. She is simply holding out her hand and offering. She doesn't take Star's approach as an invitation to interact, because it's not. This allows Star to decide whether or not proximity to the stranger is desired without suddenly being pressured into an encounter she's not ready for.

Being your dog's advocate here is a really huge thing! You might ask them put your requests for handling and how to approach Maddie in her chart so that everyone sees it before they enter the room. This has made a huge difference for Star.

Overall, it sounds like you have addressed the major approaches and you are managing the situation as well as possible. This is definitely going to be an ongoing maintenance issue. However, the more you do now the more likely that in an emergency your bank account will be high enough to tolerate some big withdrawals.

Case #4: Victor, Chihuahua, 3 years old

When did you first realize you had an issue with husbandry?

He was prone to biting from the start if he was uncomfortable with handling (loves being petted, but try to lead him by the collar and you would be bitten). He was ok at the first vet visit (nothing invasive happened) but on visit 2, I was told that I had to bring him back sedated so they could do a blood draw. We have made not much progress with this other than to train up a muzzle so that the procedure can be quick and nobody bleeds.

What, exactly, did you first notice?

He goes from zero to fighting hard as soon as he feels frightened or uncomfortable.

What did you do to try to deal with the issue?

I tried distracting him with licky mats. If I needed to address any issues with his nails, or anything else, frankly, that requires me to handle him in a way that he is not controlling.

Is it fixed, better, or ongoing?

It's better because he trusts me, but it is not good enough, and will probably be ongoing in some fashion forever. Giving him choice as much as possible has done wonders for him in general.

Recommendations:

Giving dogs a choice is powerful!

Small dogs often have issues with being handled. My personal opinion is that it's because nobody asks their permission or trains them to tolerate it; they just do it. If a giant, even a friendly one, just came along and scooped me up whenever he felt like it I'd probably bite too! So I'd start with working on a consent signal so that Victor feels like he has some say in these situations. People often worry that if they work on consent then the dog will always say "no!" This doesn't turn out to be the case though. By truly listening to our dogs and reading their signs of discomfort they will become more relaxed and tolerant, and say "yes!" much more often.

A chin rest is a nice consent signal. If Victor can maintain it then he's feeling fine but if not he's feeling uncomfortable. Work on a very strong default chin rest with lots of reinforcement. Once it's a behavior they love then it becomes a good barometer of how they are feeling.

I think that Victor would benefit from some very dedicated body handling work, first with you of course. Eventually following the sequence outlined in the book for bystanders and friendly strangers, but still with just you handling. Getting him gradually accustomed to far more vigorous handling than he's likely to get at the vet's office, and making it into a game he can win is the key to success. Right now handling is a threat. We want it to become a way to earn reinforcement. His behavior will tell you whether or not you're going slow enough with your work on body handling. If he reacts poorly then that's feedback to go back to an easier lighter level of touch, then move forward again.

Working towards Victor tolerating mild to moderate restraint would be a good long-term goal for your handling work. This may take some time because your steps need to be very small. Working on it consistently though, can lead to amazing changes in the long-run. You already realize that this is a well-established challenge and likely to be ongoing. So you have nothing to lose and everything to gain by being consistent with his handling work. Once dogs become more comfortable and feel less threatened it is pretty amazing how much they can improve.

Case #5: Rusty, Boykin Spaniel, 9 years old

When did you first realize you had an issue with husbandry?

Since he was a young dog (probably around 2 years old).

What, exactly, did you first notice?

At that time, I was having a groomer do his nails (he was my first dog and I hadn't learned how to cut nails yet). I honestly didn't realize he needed his nails trimmed so often so he was only getting them done every few months. Watching him at the groomer, he would pull his feet away from them for nail trims. Gradually it got worse to where they could barely trim them because he was flailing around so much. I decided to start doing them myself because I did not like seeing him in distress at the groomer.

What did you do to try to deal with the issue?

I tried giving him peanut butter to lick while I did his nails. This really just distracted him but didn't change his feeling about nail trims.

Is it fixed, better, or ongoing?

It is ongoing. I still usually just have someone help me and distract him with treats or peanut butter. He still is not cooperative but I haven't taken the time (nor do I have all the knowledge) to fix the problem. I typically manage the issue by just doing a foot or two at a time and then giving him a break so he doesn't get too worked up. I know they are never too old for cooperative care so I'd love to work on changing his feelings about nail trims!

I should also add that ideally I'd love to desensitize him to the dremel as I prefer that over clippers.

Recommendations:

Nails! Nails are definitely the most common challenge people have with general husbandry. Sometimes you get lucky and your dog just tolerates them, but that's not the norm. Typically, it becomes an ongoing battle that no one ever really wins.

Sometimes distraction IS enough, but not always. Your dog will let you know pretty quickly whether this quick and easy solution will work or not. However, some dogs are so food motivated that they end up in a state of great conflict. They want the food badly, but they don't want the procedure that goes along with it. If we see any signs of this happening (your dog becomes frantic or refuses the food) then we know it's time to take a different route.

Often, one of the big problems with the way people approach nails is that they are lumping (trying to do too much at once). Splitting the procedure down into small manageable chunks is a much better way to go about it.

Because the clippers have been 'poisoned' starting from scratch with the dremel is a very good idea. If introduced carefully and properly there should be no pre-existing negative connotations. The tool itself can be a new, much more pleasant experience. Where you will really need to focus your training is on counter conditioning him to leg, foot, and nail handling. This type of handling definitely has a -CER attached and so you will be starting in the hole rather than in a neutral place. It will take more work to change the response he now has than it would without the previous unpleasant experiences. But it can definitely still be changed!

I would suggest a leg/foot/nail handling plan for the long haul. Start with simply touch and treat and watch Rusty's reactions carefully. I would consider using a zen bowl with this work and see how that goes. Having the food in plain sight and easily accessible may be a big advantage here.

Splitting down leg, foot, and nail handling will take LOTS of short sessions over a period of time. There is no rush on this. Going slowly always ends up being the better choice. If Rusty shows you with his behavior that he's uncomfortable then go back to a place where he is comfortable and work forward from there.

You might also consider introducing a scratch board and shaping him to work on his own nails. This can help, especially while you're working on counter conditioning and don't want to force the issue if you don't have to.

Once a dog has developed an intense dislike of having his legs, feet, and nails handled it will likely be an ongoing issue. Once you have at least somewhat changed his mind about this there will still be regular maintenance to keep him in the land of tolerance. He'll likely never like or love it, so tolerance is a valid goal here.

k9infocus.com

If you do something & your dog objects, reinforce anyway, but use a lower level of intensity or smaller motion for the next repetition.

Start all exercises on the Floor & then move to the grooming ~~area~~ area when your dog is comfortable.

For chin rest, your dog should be facing you & either sitting or standing.
① Begin by gently placing your hand under your dogs chin. Use you calm marker, ("caaalm"), & give your dog a treat. Then repeat over & over. ② Then hold your hand an inch below & in front of dog's head. You want to see your dog move her head towards your hand, even slightly. Mark, ("caaalm"), & treat for even slightest head movement towards your hand.
Tiny steps!
Once regularly placing head in hand, you can encourage duration, by using your calm marker, ("caaalm") & feeding in position. Its okay if she moves her head away when she hears the mark, simply provide the treat so that it lures her

back into position. Most dogs quickly realise that staying in position after the marker is worthwhile because the treat is coming to that spot. It's fine for your dog to move away once she gets the treat, but if she stays in position mark & treat again. Your goal is approximately 5 seconds of duration before you move on to the specific exercises.

(Can also do two hands together & work towards muzzle wrap.)

NB. You do NOT add any verbal cue for a chin rest. Instead the cue is your open palm placed just in front of your dog as an invitation with no pressure to comply.

It's a very useful behaviour. It helps your dog learn to hold her head still. Also, as it is a voluntary behaviour, it is a very good barometer of your dogs comfort levels. It comes with lots of reinforcement, so if once learnt thoroughly, dog chooses not to, its an excellent indicator that they are not comfortable with whats going on.

You should also teach a chin rest to a pillow or towel in your lap, or on a stool or chair for when you need both hands free.

Impulse Control

Two markers — "Caaalm"
& "Take it"

Slow. (treats from shoulder height);
Zen bowl ; Zen hand (open, close, fist) ; Food on floor).
(Go slowly — tiny steps . I often have gone
at far too too great a speed of change & in
all training need to change things by much
smaller, gradual increments. Rushing will get
us nowhere fast !)

· General body handling — Start with very gentle
stroking to find out sensitive areas.
Stroke dog lightly, use your calm marker whilst you a
still stroking, then give your dog a treat.
All your dog has to do is hold still & allow
stroking to happen, but in the initial stages, doesn't
need to hold still completely . If he moves away
mark & treat anyway .
Avoid talking (as much as possible), other
than use of calm marker .

Pushing — aim is for body to yield & move. Flat ha

Poking — aim to hold still)

Pinching — eg upper back leg .

See pg 53

Restraint   eg. body;
                    & head; etc.

Lifting   pg   56

Standing → needs very high rate of reinforcement.

Lie down on the side — see pg. 58.

Rolling onto back.

Bathtime → less important as we have ways
but good to teach. Use bath mats &
wade ballpool, clear plastic tub.

(checklist pg. 65)

Muzzle training pg. 76

* For blood draw, nervous dogs often
better with it taken from hind leg
so vet isn't in their face.

See checklist pg. 80 for head work.

Footwork pg. 85.

Tools pg. 97.
(vets)

Core pg. 102.

People & places pg. 107.

Printed in Poland
by Amazon Fulfillment
Poland Sp. z o.o., Wrocław

54555227R00078